MY FAVORITE

PRAYER STORIES

JOE L. WHEELER

Pacific Press®
Publishing Association
Nampa, Idaho | Oshawa, Ontario, Canada
www.pacificpress.com

Cover design by Gerald Lee Monks
Cover illustration from Marcus Mashburn
Interior design by Aaron Troia

Copyright © 2015 by
Pacific Press® Publishing Association
Printed in the United States of America
All rights reserved

The author assumes full responsibility for the accuracy
of all facts and quotations as cited in this book.

Visit Joe Wheeler's Web site at: www.joewheelerbooks
.com. None of these stories may be reprinted or placed
on the Internet without the express written permission
of the editor/compiler, Joe L. Wheeler (P.O. Box 1246,
Conifer, CO 80433), or the copyright holder.

The quotations, other than Scripture, on the section
dividers in this book are from Philip Yancey's book
Prayer: Does It Make Any Difference? (Grand Rapids,
MI: Zondervan, 2006).

Scripture quotations marked NLT are taken from the
Holy Bible, New Living Translation, copyright © 2004,
2007, 2013 by Tyndale House Foundation. Used by
permission of Tyndale House Publishers, Inc., Carol
Stream, Illinois 60188 All rights reserved. (This book
uses the NLT 2007.)

Scripture texts credited to NRSV are from the New
Revised Standard Version of the Bible, copyright ©
1989 by the Division of Christian Education of the
National Council of the Churches of Christ in the
U.S.A. Used by permission. All rights reserved.

You can obtain additional copies of this book by calling
toll-free 1-800-765-6955 or by visiting
http://www.adventistbookcenter.com.

Library of Congress Cataloging-in-Publication Data
  My favorite prayer stories / Joe L. Wheeler.
      pages cm
   ISBN 978-0-8163-5897-7 (pbk.)
1. Prayer--Christianity. I. Title.
   BV220.W43 2016
   242—dc23

                                          2015035434

December 2015

DEDICATION

One of the best and longest-running youth magazines ever published was *The Youth's Instructor*. Founded by James White in 1852, it lasted until 1970.

The editor of that magazine who was most loved by two generations of young people (including mine) came on board in 1911, became associate editor in 1918 and chief editor in 1923, remaining in that position until 1952. Thus her influence was felt for forty-one years!

During my growing-up years, hers was a household name in our home, for the magazine faithfully arrived every week, and we read it from cover to cover. Her weekly column, "Let's Talk It Over," was widely clipped, quoted from, and used in worship services everywhere. She loved the deeply moving Christian stories that she borrowed from other Christian magazines of the time. I've since discovered that during that period there was a close-knit group of Christian editors who shamelessly borrowed from each other, sometimes giving credit source-wise, and sometimes not. However, until I began the *My Favorite . . .* story series, I hadn't realized that, like her contemporaries, this editor had anthologized a treasure chestful of truly inspirational stories.

If you look in the acknowledgments section of the books in this series, you'll see what a debt of gratitude we owe her. In our seventy-six story anthologies, no other editor is responsible for anywhere near as many spiritually based story inclusions as was

LORA E. CLEMENT
(1890–1958).

CONTENTS

THE UPS AND DOWNS OF PRAYER LIFE

Thirty-one years ago in an article titled "My Prayer Journal,"[1] I attempted to capture in all too frail words the essence of my prayer life. But that was *then*. I've discovered since then that my prayer life is constantly changing. It changes because every day *I* change. What worked yesterday will not necessarily work today.

As I reflect on my journal, I ruefully discover that my prayer life is weakest when everything appears to be going right and strongest when I'm driven to my knees by the perception that things are caving in around me. It is all these roller-coasterish undulations (exhilarating ascents to the top, and sobering plunges to the bottom) that make it impossible for me to arrive at a template that can serve as a model for others.

Philip Yancey, in his powerful *Prayer: Does It Make Any Difference?* phrases it this way: "We pray because we want to thank someone or something for the beauties and glories of life, and also because we feel small and helpless and sometimes afraid. We pray for forgiveness, for strength, for contact with the One who is, for assurance that we are not alone. Millions in AA groups pray daily to a Higher Power, begging for help in controlling their addictions. We pray because we can't help it."[2]

I've also discovered that my prayer life is strongly affected by the eternal tug of war between pride and humility in my life. When pride is in the ascendancy, prayer is relegated to a back seat. Humility, however, is a soulmate to prayer. No matter how many times I stuff pride back in its box and lock the lid, it's such a Houdinian escape artist that it always discovers a way to get back out. I may win battlefield victories over pride, but the war will continue until the day I die.

How Should We Pray?

Another discovery I've made over time is that nothing works very long. When I inaugurated my prayer journal in 1983, I blithely assumed I'd arrived at a prayer formula that would work from then on. I hadn't taken into consideration how quickly even prayer can become stale. The problem is that I must not take God for granted. What that means is that unless my prayer life is fresh every day, it quickly becomes stale and ineffective. And the problem with prayer checklists is the astonishing rapidity with which they, too, deteriorate into perfunctory staleness. Once my prayers deteriorate into prayer-wheelish rote, they struggle to get any higher than the ceiling of my room.

Which brings me to *how* I pray. I'd always assumed that closed eyes was a prerequisite to effective prayer—so much so that subconsciously I considered my wife's open-eyed praying to be not only ineffective but more than a little sacrilegious. The holiest of all prayer attitudes had to be that of kneeling down with eyes closed. So imagine the shock as I read this:

> Some pray-ers feel constrained by the body language of praying. Should we kneel? Close our eyes? Use a formal or casual approach? What is the appropriate prayer *style*?

The Bible itself includes a multitude of styles. Peter knelt, Jeremiah stood, Nehemiah sat down, Abraham prostrated himself , and Elijah put his face between his knees. In Jesus' day most Jews stood, lifting their open eyes to heaven. The Virgin Mary prayed in poetry. Paul interspersed his prayers with singing.[3]

Yancey concludes that there can be no one way to pray. What counts is the sincerity of the one praying. The several hundred prayer stories I've read have confirmed this. However, some petitioners borderline demand that God come through for them. It has only been in recent years that I have discovered that God rarely answers "gimme" prayers—first and foremost because He respects us so much that He refuses to invade our will. Only when we phrase our prayer "Not my will but Thine be done" (Catherine Marshall calls this the "prayer of relinquishment") does God feel free to step in. Yet, depending on the supplicant's attitude, motive, or need, God will often respond positively to straight request prayers.

Sweeping Biblical Promises

It is likely that no other aspect of prayer has caused more confusion than Jesus' promises that whatever we ask for in His name will be granted. Yancey wrestled with this issue but was not able to come to a clear-cut conclusion. Even the Bible features many unanswered prayers—and delayed-fuse prayers and prayers that God answers with an outright No.

Yancey finally turned to one possibility that was new to me:

> How can we reconcile the lavish promises with the actual experience of so many sincere Christians who struggle with unanswered prayer? One possible explanation centers in the specific group of people whom Jesus was addressing: the disciples. Could it be that Jesus gave the Twelve, handpicked to carry on the work after his death, certain rights and privileges in prayer that would not be normative for every follower? The Gospel writers do not explicitly say "These commands apply to the disciples only," but they do specify in each case that Jesus was speaking to his intimate disciples, not a large crowd.[4]

Yancey also points out that virtually all of these pronouncements contain the qualifier that such requests will not only be in the name of God but also compatible with His will. Might not some of our prayer requests be perhaps a bit frivolous?

In this vein, almost all of the stories in this collection have to do with God's saying Yes. All of us know that Yes prayers are anything but the norm; however, believers have written very few No stories. This absence so bothered me that as I made the final slate of stories a matter of continuous prayer, I was convicted that I should include one particular story that addresses this issue: Jeanette Swing's "The Other Boy."

In conclusion, I firmly believe that prayers are not meant merely to supply our wants, although God does grant a surprisingly large number of such prayers. Rather, they are meant to deepen our friendship and companionship with our Maker.

Any who would like to dig deeper into the subject of prayer would find studying Yanc-ey's prayerful book to be not only inspirational but faith-affirming.

Coda

I would love to hear from you what your reaction to these stories has been. You may even be able to track down the authors of some of the old stories, or even descendants of those authors. You may reach me at

Joe L. Wheeler, Ph.D.
P.O. Box 1246
Conifer, CO 80433

---

1. Joe L. Wheeler, "My Prayer Journal," *Signs of the Times,* August 1985.
2. Philip Yancey, *Prayer: Does It Make Any Difference?* (Grand Rapids, MI: Zondervan, 2006), 13.
3. Ibid., 191, 192.
4. Ibid., 235.

SECTION ONE

"You don't have what you want because you don't ask God for it, and even when you ask, you don't get it because your motives are all wrong—you want only what will give you pleasure."
—James 4:2, 3; NLT

"Prayers of request tend to fall into one of two categories: trouble or trivia. As if by instinct we cry out to God when trouble strikes."
—Yancey, page 73

*T*his story has been patiently waiting for half a century in my story archives. Waiting until, in His own good time, God would will that the time of its publishing had come at last.

Significantly, it took the pastor half a century before he shared this epiphany with Marcus Bach—thus the story has had more than a hundred-year fuse.

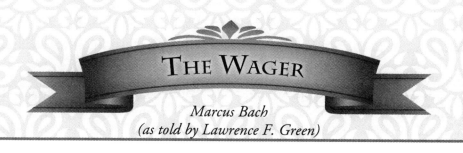

THE WAGER

Marcus Bach
(as told by Lawrence F. Green)

At a religious conference in California I met a retired clergyman, Lawrence F. Green, of Stockton. I said to him, "In looking back over your fifty years in the ministry, what stands out as your greatest experience?"

He replied at once, "That day I preached the sermon God told me to preach."

It happened during the early days of his first pastorate in a wide-open western town in North Dakota, a frontier town full of "blind pigs," gamblers, and gunmen who defied the law.

One Monday as young Pastor Green sat down to outline a sermon for the next week's church service, he visualized, as he had done often before, his struggling congregation of well-intentioned parishioners. It was a small flock of thirty-five who came regularly to the services, listened to his words, and tried as best they could to "live the life." This Monday, as always, the minister selected a text he was quite sure would serve: "Blessed are the meek, for they shall inherit the earth."

As he reflected on these words, it seemed as if he heard a voice saying to him, "What about the people who aren't meek and who never come to church? Preach to them for a change. Don't preach about the meek. Preach Galatians 6:7."

Pastor Green turned the pages of his Bible to the text in Galatians that says, "Be not deceived; God is not mocked: for whatsoever a man soweth, that shall he also reap." All that week he struggled with the question of whether he truly had heard the voice of God speaking to him.

When the night before he was to preach came he was in such a quandary that he went to his study and dropped to his knees. "O God," he prayed, "if You want me to preach a sermon from that text, it is up to You to send the people to church who never ordinarily come. If you will send them to the service, I will preach whatever You want me to say."

As he prayed he could hear the Saturday night sounds with their usual note of noise and violence. The first automobile had just been introduced in town, and drunken horseback riders were daring the automobile driver to race with them. Over the commotion came the bellowing voice of pistol-toting Big Tim who was once more running afoul of the law and vociferously arguing with the sheriff.

Pastor Green listened in his study as he gazed down at Galatians 6:7. "If the people come," he said half-aloud, "I will use that text." Was God given to bargaining? He did not know. There were many things his years of training for the ministry had not revealed to him. But he could not doubt that he had heard a voice and that something in his heart said, "There is a sermon God wants you to preach."

Where was the sermon? For the first time in his career he had nothing written out on the eve of the Sabbath. No notes. No outline. It was a new experience and an awkward one, a kind of "wrestling with an angel."

Sunday came. After breakfast he went to his study to select the hymns and a Scripture reading. He also recited his customary morning prayer, but running through his mind like a thundering herd were the words "Preach that sermon!"

As he left the parsonage with his wife, she asked, "What are you preaching about this morning?"

"I don't know," he said.

"You don't know?" she exclaimed. "What do you mean?"

"I don't have a sermon," he replied. "Today the Lord must truly put the words into my mouth."

His wife, sensing his concern, said quietly, "I am sure He will."

They made their way to the simple white-frame steepled church as they had many times before. This morning things seemed different. This Sabbath was uncommonly quiet. There was a somber feeling about this overcast morning, and the clang of the church bell sounded like an alarm. The customary, "Good morning, pastor," and "Well, here it is Sunday again" went almost unheard. What Pastor Green remembered most was the reassuring touch of his wife's hand and her confident words, "I am sure He will."

He walked slowly up the narrow center aisle to the pulpit and seated himself in the high-backed chair while the woman at the portable organ played her customary prelude. He closed his eyes, carrying in his vision the people in the pews. They were his usual flock, the folks who always came. He knew them well. They were the meek. They were his people.

So, Lord, he said to himself while the organ played, *here we are as we have been many times before. I thought that today a kind of miracle might happen. I felt it in my soul that this morning would be something special, but we are here as usual.*

Meditating along these lines, he suddenly heard a sound above the organ's tones. In the church yard a number of galloping horses were slowing to a halt. There were voices outside the door, loud voices that soon dropped to a respectful whisper. Then he heard a shuffling of feet down the aisles of the church. He fought back an impulse to open his eyes. In his innermost mind he knew what was happening: God was keeping His part of the bargain.

He opened his eyes and saw a congregation such as he had never seen before. The meek and lowly had been joined by more than seventy of the bold and haughty! They sat there dressed as for a Saturday night, men and women who had never been in church, not even for a funeral. They were here now, and as he asked them to rise for the invocation he stood face to face with his own terms. Even while he prayed aloud, another prayer was going through his mind: *O God, give me the strength and the words to fulfill my part of the bargain we have made!*

His parishioners gazed at him as if asking what magic had lured these non-churchgoers to the service or what plot they might be hatching by their presence. He caught a reassuring glance from his wife that reflected his own thought: *they are here because God brought them.*

Then there was a restless stir. Big Tim, six-foot-six and wearing his pistol belt over his cowboy togs, had entered. Big Tim sauntered up the center aisle and took a place next to a most respectable elderly woman parishioner. With remarkable politeness, she handed him an open hymnal, and Big Tim stood there book in hand while the people sang, "Safely through another week, Thou hast brought us on our way."

The time came for the sermon. As Pastor Green slowly turned the pages of the large pulpit Bible, his affection for the Lord and His Word became a fellow-feeling for all people. He had looked for an opportunity to lay down the law, but now he wanted only a chance to remind men of God's love.

"Dear friends," he heard himself say, "our text for today is found in Galatians 6:7, where we read, 'Be not deceived; God is not mocked: for whatsoever a man soweth, that shall he also reap.'"

Several of the meek caught their breath and glanced about uneasily, but under his gaze they finally decided he might also have included them in this unflinching text.

"God," Pastor Green proclaimed, "is saying to us here that we ourselves set the judgment of our own souls. He is warning us that our sins will find us out and that the things we do fashion our lives and the lives of others. God, as we all know, hates sin but loves the sinner. He sees something of Himself in every man. He sees Himself in you and me because we are made in His image. The more power and authority He gives a man, the more He expects that man to do His will, and that goes for Big Tim here as well as for me."

For the first time in his ministry Pastor Green was speaking as men of Bible times must have spoken when they were "in the spirit." For once the people listened as though waiting his command. They sat in agreement as he cited the lawlessness and evil rampant in the community. They heard him warn Big Tim of "the fearful harvest that must be reaped if the seeds of sin continue to be sown." They saw through his eyes how a loving Father denounced wickedness and longed for order and peace.

"This day," he prophesied, "God has come to our town to triumph over evil and to transfer the bent toward violence into a force for good. For if our freedom leads only to license, think what cowards we must be in His sight!"

The organist was so absorbed she forgot to play the response after the sermon-prayer. For once the people wanted their pastor to keep on speaking after the appointed time. Even the benediction was different. "God," said Pastor Green, "has brought us here this morning to enter into a new covenant with Him this day."

When he went to the door to shake hands with the people, he was tempted to ask every visitor, "What put it into your heart to come this morning?" He especially wanted to ask Big Tim, but he refrained. The time had come to trust and believe. So he grasped each hand and said, "God bless you." Big Tim responded, "Bless you, too, Parson. You preached just what we came to hear."

There were tears in the eyes of his parishioners as they tarried after church-time. One man said in a shaky voice, "This is what I've been praying for." A woman told Pastor Green, "I knew this would happen someday." Mrs. Green put her hand in his and said, "Neither we nor others will ever be the same after today."

That was literally true. Throughout the town and for miles around, people talked about the sermon, about the miracle of attendance, and about the changes that were already beginning to be felt in individual lives.

On Wednesday, which was mail day, Pastor Green went to the post office. Here everyone commented on the "Galatian Sermon," but it was the postmaster who took him aside and said, "Say, pastor, Big Tim said your sermon was such a humdinger that he is going to help clean up the town and cooperate with the sheriff in enforcing the law—and Big Tim always keeps his word. Do you know why he came to the service and why all the other folks came along? Big Tim lost a gambling bet, that's why. Lost it late the night before you preached. After practically losing his shirt he said to those who were crowding around the table, 'If I lose this next poker hand, danged if I don't go to church in the morning!' He lost all right and everybody came to church to see whether he'd really be there. Oh, he always keeps his word."

"You can say he came to church because of the gambling debt," said Pastor Green doggedly, "but God knew that Big Tim and all the rest of them were coming to church as long ago as last *Monday morning!*"

"How come?" exclaimed the postmaster. "It just happened last night."

"Because that's just the way the good Lord works," said Pastor Green, and then he turned and walked thoughtfully away. ❧

*M*any years ago, when I was a boy, I spent several weeks at Wawona Junior Camp near Yosemite. While there, a large group of us took a two-day hike. The first evening, I spread out my sleeping bag a little apart from the others near a large tree. Next morning, even before I had awakened, other campers had discovered some large tracks: in a small circle all around me were mountain lion tracks. What kept the maker of those tracks from ending my young life? I'll never know the answer until I reach the kingdom.

Real Courage

Laura Nelson

We have enough for breakfast now," called Don. "Let's go and get the fire started and the flapjacks mixed before the boys wake up."

Donald Simms and Lynn Gorton were part of a group of boys on a camping trip in the mountains. They had "rolled out" at five o'clock and gone in search of wild strawberries for breakfast as a surprise on the menu.

Lynn handed Don the basket of luscious crimson berries and began searching for kindling. In a few minutes he had a fire crackling and was vigorously beating the pancake batter while Don hulled the berries. The busy clatter awakened the boys in the tent. Leaping from their cots, they hurried into their clothes and were ready for breakfast by the time the first skillet of golden-brown flapjacks was ready for them.

Lynn had been reared in the mountains, and he loved the out-of-doors. He had had few contacts with people, having spent most of his life miles away from any town. His companions had always been the animals, the flowers, the trees. But he had completed the grammar school near his home, and for the past nine months had had the new experience of living among strangers in a school dormitory. As he had never before had the privilege of such close companionship with other boys, he was ill at ease in such a crowd. His timidity had led some of the boys to make sport of the "country greenhorn," as they laughingly called him. This made him even more shy and self-conscious. But he was anxious to make his school career a success and spent much time diligently studying.

Don was a junior in the academy. He was studious, dependable, always ready to lend a helping hand, and was highly respected by his classmates. He had been very kind to Lynn and had done all he could to make the mountain boy feel at home in his new surroundings. In fact, he had often remonstrated with his friends for making fun of the newcomer.

Walter Powell, another member of the camping crowd, was popular and self-confident, a leader among the boys in merrymaking—often at Lynn's expense. His glossy black hair, slicked back above his well-molded features, was in direct contrast to Lynn's unruly shock that topped a generously freckled face. It seemed that in everything the boys were exact opposites.

At the close of the school term, a group of boys, including Don and Walter, secured from their parents permission to spend two weeks camping in the mountains before returning home. The spot chosen for the camp was not far from where Lynn lived, and at Don's invitation, he often went with them on their hikes. These were familiar surroundings to him, and his bashfulness dropped away as a useless cloak, and he joined wholeheartedly in the fun. Last night he had stayed, yielding to special urging, and now morning found him up early, "helping the cook."

"Let's go for a hike today," suggested Jack, as pancakes and berries disappeared with amazing rapidity.

Enthusiasm greeted the suggestion, and breakfast over, the boys quickly put the camp in order and tramped out the fire. Then, with Don and Lynn in the lead, they set out, provisions for lunch bulging from their pockets.

In fact, each day that they had been in the woods, the boys, with the exception of Walter, had looked more and more to Lynn

for guidance. And modestly, yet with a certain unconscious dignity, he accepted the trust. Being on home ground, he was sure of himself. Rather than be left alone, Walter followed his lead, but grudgingly and ungraciously.

Along the mountain paths they trudged, stopping now and again to examine some unusual shrub or to enjoy the panorama of the valley spread out below them. At noon Lynn called a halt, and the boys prepared the lunch over the crackling fire he quickly built.

After lunch and a short rest, the hikers were ready for the return tramp.

"Let's go back by a different path," suggested Walter.

Lynn hesitated. "There is another path," he admitted, "but it takes us over some very dangerous ground."

"Adventure is just what we want," quickly insisted Walter, who disliked letting this "greenhorn from the woods" think he could do something that the rest could not. "Lead on," he said. "Wherever you go, we will follow."

Though the path was rougher and steeper than they had anticipated, the boys did follow uncomplainingly, making their way single file in and out among the trees and over boulders.

Finally Lynn stopped, and turning to the group following, explained, "We have just this canyon left to cross. Over that rise is camp. But this canyon is rocky, and the path is very steep, and the footing not very sure. So be careful."

And careful the boys were—so careful that they were nearly across the treacherous trail when a stone slipped under Walter's foot. Down the steep side of the ravine he plunged, landing about ten feet below the path with his left leg doubled beneath him.

Don and Lynn scrambled down and raised him up, but his left leg had been broken, and he could not stand. Then Lynn tied the rope which he had carried, fearing some such emergency, around the injured boy's waist, and climbing down the ledge beside him, he supported Walter as his companions hoisted him up again to the path. Then making a packsaddle, they carried their unfortunate pal to camp.

But what was to be done now? Walter must have help without delay. The excited boys discussed their next move.

"How can we get Walt out, and where's the nearest doctor?" demanded Don. "And it took us two days to get here!" he groaned.

"We'll *have* to get help," decided Lynn calmly. "There's a forest ranger's station eight miles away. I'll go over there and telephone for horses and a doctor."

"But you can't go through these woods at night," exclaimed Don. "Remember those bear tracks we saw today—and there are plenty of other wild animals too."

"I'm not afraid," Lynn assured the boys, and added reverently, "God will go with me."

No one could dissuade him from this course—to tell the truth, they did not try very hard, as they saw Walter's suffering. But not one of them had the courage to offer to go with Lynn.

Dusk was approaching as Lynn set out. The path lay before him dark and mysterious, but he was a good woodsman, and without hesitation struck out rapidly, making surprising progress through the quiet forest.

Snap! The sound of a twig breaking some distance to the right broke the stillness. Again, some moments later, the same sound came from ahead of the lone boy. Every nerve in his body grew tense, but he pushed steadily forward, walking as fast as possible. In a few moments the snapping of a twig on his left confirmed his suspicions—a mountain lion was following him!

With a whispered prayer, Lynn asked God to protect him from this danger and to allow him to fulfill his mission and bring help for his stricken comrade. Then, peering intently into the darkness, he quickened his pace, but dared not run.

The crackling of the brush made by the stealthy march of the prowler told Lynn that the lion was walking around him in a large circle. It was still fully a mile to the ranger's cabin. Could he make it? Round and round him the lion crept, making each circle smaller than the preceding one.

As the radius of that circle diminished, Lynn walked faster and faster. Could he reach the forester's cabin before the lion got close enough to spring? He was frightened—terribly frightened. He prayed constantly. Well did he realize his own helplessness, his absolute and utter dependence upon his heavenly Father.

It seemed to Lynn that he had gone *miles* at that furious pace. In vain his eyes searched for the light of the cabin he knew must be near, but he could see only deep blackness on all sides of him. Then he heard the soft padding of the mountain lion's paws. How close the animal was! He knew that the beast might spring at almost any moment now. The boy steeled himself for the conflict just as his long strides led him to a clearing, and the light from the ranger's cabin, only a few yards ahead of him, burst on his grateful gaze. He was safe! A leap for the door, and he stumbled inside.

The astonished ranger sprang to his feet at this unceremonious entrance of a visitor, but before he could say a word the boy dropped to his knees, and in a voice shaking with emotion, thanked his kind heavenly Father for deliverance. Then, his prayer of thanksgiving concluded, Lynn told of the accident on the trail, but insisted on telephoning for help before telling of his own danger and narrow escape.

The ranger could hardly believe his story. "I don't understand why the lion played with you so long and then let you get away," he pondered. "You're certainly lucky to be alive!"

"God's hand was holding the lion," declared Lynn reverently, "and he couldn't spring because God wouldn't let him. I'm alive because God wanted me to be alive!"

Two weeks later Walter lay in a hammock under the shady trees surrounding Lynn's home. His leg was in a cast and healing steadily. As "the country greenhorn" approached, he looked up and spoke earnestly. "Lynn, I'll never forget what a pal you have been—and after the way I've treated you! The doctor says I can go home in a week. And as soon as I can get around without crutches, I want you to come and visit me. My dad thinks you're great, and the rest of the folks at home'll be glad to meet you too. I can hardly wait to introduce a *fellow who isn't afraid of anything!*" ❧

*I*n my own life, I'm almost embarrassed to admit how often I've asked God for such trivial things—like lost glasses, misplaced this and that, a name I've forgotten, something on my to-do list that I forgot to write down, and on and on.
The amazing thing is that not only does He not mind, He answers those prayers!

Wendy Miller

My kids looked forward to the 5-Day Club that was to be held in my friend's backyard. She did it every summer. Through stories and songs she taught about God's love. There were crafts to do, verses to memorize, and, at the end of the five days, prizes to be won.

My friend's house wasn't far, and my kids knew the way so I would just send them out the door and then bask in the quietness that is rarely heard when you have four small children. Usually I would clean my house, which may sound like an odd way to enjoy oneself, but I enjoyed the satisfaction of seeing it stay that way for one whole hour.

On one of the days it happened to be raining so I drove the kids to the club. We arrived a little early, so I went in to chat for a moment with my friend. When the rest of the children arrived I turned to go.

"You're welcome to stay if you like," my friend said.

I thought for a moment. Why not? I had planned to vacuum the house, but I found I had no vacuum bags. Money was scarce in those days. I had emptied the bag I had been using over and over again. But it had been repaired so many times that on that day it finally just fell apart. I had been so frustrated and angry. Well, I would stay. It seemed I had nothing better to do.

I flopped down into a chair at the back of the room and let my mind drift back and forth between the class and my own problems. When story time began I perked up to listen. The story was about a young boy who needed to buy soap. His clothes were dirty, and he wanted to wash them but he didn't have enough money to buy soap. Even the cheapest bar was a dollar, and he had only fifty cents. So he prayed and told the Lord about his problem and asked for help. Then he went to the store and there he found some soap that was on sale for fifty cents a bar.

I couldn't believe my ears. What kind of junk was he trying to teach my kids! I was a

Christian, and I believed in the power of prayer, but there was no way that the Almighty God is going to give a hoot about something as inconsequential as soap!

Look at me, I thought. *I have only five dollars, and I know that my vacuum bags cost ten dollars. Kind of the same situation, but there is no way that I would bother to pray about it. There are too many big problems in the world for Him to look after. He does not concern Himself with trivial matters.* I politely waited for the hour to be up and then packed my kids up in the car to drive home.

I was totally absorbed in my thoughts and had my brain on automatic pilot as I drove. When I came back to the real world, I realized that I had driven to the mall instead of home. I decided that wandering the mall might be a good way to spend the rainy afternoon after all.

In the mall I passed a small store that sold reconditioned vacuum cleaners. I stopped in front of it, and my mind drifted back to the story. I must have stood there for a long time because the owner of the shop stepped to the door and asked if I wanted something.

I was embarrassed. "Only if you have a half-price sale on vacuum bags," I said and then laughed. I knew he didn't. I had been there often enough to know that his prices were already low and he never had a sale on anything.

"Actually, I do in a way," he said in return. "A lady was just in here and somehow talked me into selling her half a package. I have the other half behind the counter. They're yours for five dollars."

I could almost hear God's voice. "Did you really think I didn't care? Don't you know that I can do anything at all? I care about even the smallest part of your life. About soap and bags. Even the hairs on your head are all numbered."

Wow, what a lesson! And I thought the 5-Day Club was for kids. ❧

*T*wo minutes—that's how long the missionary's prayer lasted. We have seen, again and again in these stories, God responding to short prayers—some as short as two or three minutes. So, the length is not the determining factor—especially when the petitioner is in such immediate danger that lengthy prayers are all but impossible.

A CRY FOR HELP IN THE JUNGLE

William Butler
and W. A. Spicer

William Butler, founder of the Methodist missions in India, was fleeing from Bareli, north India, with his wife and little ones. The terrifying news of the Sepoy mutiny at Meerut and then at Delhi had come, and no time was to be lost in getting to Naini Tal, a European hill station in the Himalaya Mountains. Native bearers were engaged to carry the doolies (palanquins). In these rode Mrs. Butler, whose health was precarious, and the two children, with the baggage.

They had entered the Terai, a jungle region at the foot of the mountains "reeking with malaria, and the haunt of tigers and elephants," Dr. Butler, in his *Land of the Vedas*, says. "The rank vegetation stood in places like high walls on either side. At midnight we reached that part of it where the bearers are changed. The other palanquins had their full complement of men; but of the twenty-nine bearers for whom I paid, I could find only nine men and one torch-bearer; and this, too, in such a place!

"Darkness and tigers were around us; the other palanquins were starting one after another, each with its torch to frighten away the beasts, the bearers taking advantage of the rush to extort heavy baksheesh."

Rendered desperate, Dr. Butler put the two children in one palanquin with Mrs. Butler. He ran after a man with a cart, who was disappearing up the road, and compelled him to turn his bullocks and take on board the servant Ann and the little baggage they were taking in their flight.

Then the doctor turned to watch the bearers start on with Mrs. Butler and the children. But not one stirred. "They were exhausted by extra work, and might have even fairly refused to carry two children with a lady; and to have taken either of them on the bullock cart was impossible. Delay seemed ruinous to the only plan by which I could get them on at all.

If the men refused the burden, and left, they would take with them, for their own protection, the only torch there was, which belonged to them, and we should have been left in darkness, exposed to the tigers and the deadly malaria. . . .

"It was an awful moment. For a few minutes my agony was unutterable; I thought I had done all I could, and now everything was on the brink of failure. I saw how 'vain' was 'the help of man,' and I turned aside into the dark jungle, took off my hat, and lifted my heart to God. If ever I prayed, I prayed then. I besought God in mercy to influence the hearts of these men, and decide for me in that solemn hour. I reminded Him of the mercies that had hitherto followed us, and implored His interference in this emergency. My prayer did not last two minutes, but how I prayed in that time!

"I put on my hat, returned to the light, and looked. I spoke not; I saw my men at once bend to the dooly; it rose, and off they went instantly, and they never stopped a moment, except kindly to push little Eddie in, when in his sleep he rolled so that his feet hung out."

On they went through the dark night, and on through the jungle, and out at last into the safety of the mountain passes. Dr. Butler knew that it was the Lord's own interference that had turned the hearts of those heathen coolies when he had exhausted every human resource in vain.

"God is the refuge of His saints,
When storms of sharp distress invade." ❧

*D*uring the Great Depression, the first victims were job holders, who were let go. The second victims were those so essential to the company that they couldn't function without them. These, though they were retained, had to do double the work at half salary or less. The money to pay them more was just not there.

WHITE WALLS

Gussie Ross Jobe

I've grown to hate the very sight of them—those high white walls! The house of pain, I call it; they oppress me with their immaculate grimness—those terrible, cold white walls." Bee faltered and then went on. "The tragedies that take place behind them—the sorrow and pain. I dread going to work. I want to turn and run from them."

"Why, Bee darling!" her mother's voice was gently distressed. "Do you feel well? You've never spoken like this before. You need a vacation."

"Vacation?" Bee laughed mirthlessly. "That word is obsolete these days, especially at St. Matthew's Hospital—what with every girl doubling for someone they can let go, and doing that for almost nothing. It has been six months since we have been paid full salary—half pay indeed! We have paid the landlord and the grocer half of what we owe them as long as we can. We will just have to find cheaper quarters—take two rooms in some *dump!*"

"Perhaps that *would* be wise, darling."

"But think of poor Grandmother—make her give up the comforts she has here: furnace heat in winter, her sun porch and garden, the view, the breeze from the lake . . . Oh, I couldn't *think* of moving her. She won't be with us so very much longer, and I'd put up with anything to make her last days comfortable and cheerful."

"Hush, darling. You have been so brave and good to the two helpless old women dependent upon you. I feel sure that a way will open. Have you prayed about it?"

Bee's pretty young face twisted wryly. "Motherkin, the days of answered prayers are over—if they ever existed. No, I've never had the temerity to call upon the Almighty for assistance when I see so much greater suffering that needs His attention within those great white walls."

"But think how much more suffering there would be without them. Prayer—"

"You do it, dearest, pray for us all, especially poor Grandmother Glenn."

"I *do* pray for her, Bee, and I bear in mind that she has always prayed for me—for us—"

"And are her prayers always answered?" Bee sat still a long time waiting for her mother to answer.

"It is strange, dear, that you should speak of white walls—"

From her huge winged chair upon the sun porch, little withered Grandmother Glenn stirred restlessly among the bright Navaho rugs that incased her like a mummy. Her sight was dim and her memory wandered, but her hearing was still faultless, and as the conversation drifted to her ears, she drew her dreaming spirit from the happy, golden past and tried to concentrate upon what they were saying. She heard talk of answered prayers and the words "white walls."

What was this nonsense Bee was speaking? God did not answer prayers? She pressed her tiny, gnarled fingers to her white hair and tried to think what this awakened in her memory, for she was apt to confuse the past with the present. She wavered between the two in a pleasant haze.

White walls? Ah, yes, now she remembered. She laid her white head back against the cushions, her eyes closed. The glittering jade of the distant lake faded from her memory and in its place arose a small farmhouse. Grandmother drifted back on the wings of dreams.

It was such a tiny farm, but it had taken every cent of big Zeke's savings to buy it for a wedding present for pretty Kitty Spaulding. Five dollars an acre and uncultivated, but rich, sandy bottom land. They had cleared it and built a two-room frame house. Those first few years had been wonderful even though they were fraught with hardship—wonderful, because these hardships had been wrestled with and overcome. It had been their enduring determination to establish a home that would shelter them through the years of rearing the two babies that eventually made their appearance— sturdy little Chappy and sweet baby Sue.

After a few years of searing summer heat and the cold of long winters, the little place took on a home-like aspect. The acres were fertile and under Kitty's skillful hands looked homey and lovely. And the children were sweet and unspoiled. There was every incentive to carry on—but then the war broke out.

Poor Zeke was torn between home and duty, and Kitty wanted him to be uninfluenced by her opinion. After weighing the matter pro and con, Zeke finally volunteered, and was rejected because of a lame foot, injured when the house was built.

Kitty could not help being overjoyed, and Zeke was relieved that the matter had been taken from his hands. A great contentment pervaded the little home. They were going to be cozy and happy that winter, and they went about the business of preparing for it with peace in their hearts.

Then came a tricky day in midwinter—the sun was pale and watery, hiding sometimes behind dark gray clouds, only to pop out now and again in a half-hearted attempt to shine. A restlessness of the wind foretold a weather change—a regular "weather breeder" of a day.

Kitty sang as she worked. Inside the little house all was bustle and cheer. Before the fireplace, in which burned fragrant apple wood, stood an iron crane, with a three-legged black pot suspended upon it. The cornmeal pudding within it simmered and erupted tiny volcanoes of fragrant steam.

On the floor near the woodbox little Chappy was building a corral of white corncobs. The animals corralled inside were represented by glossy brown buckeyes. In the corner of the kitchen was a bed, moved here for greater convenience and warmth during the extreme weather. On this bed sat little Sue, crooning over a dolly made of winter squash. True, the dolly's neck was extremely swan-like and her face—fashioned by Zeke's penknife—was rather flat, but was she not wrapped around with Mother's bright paisley shawl? Certainly. To Sue she was the loveliest doll in the whole world.

Kitty thumped the dasher of the churn up and down, up and down. Small clots of golden butter began to appear and cling to the dasher; the butter was coming early today, and Kitty was glad. There would be time to cool the pudding, mold and slice it, and fry it in butter. With some of Zeke's smooth sorghum and the new buttermilk, what a feast they would have! So Kitty sang because she was happy and because it amused the children. She sang, stopping now and again to give them exaggerated gestures:

"Pompeii was dead, and he lay in
his grave—
    Laid in his grave—laid in his
grave—"

She ended each line with a long-drawn-out "O-o-h," in which the children joined with many giggles.

The fire snapped and popped, foretelling snow. Kitty moved her treasured geranium, brought all the way from her home in Missouri. If it should freeze tonight—but she'd remember to cover it.

Getting out the wooden bowl, she swirled

the mass of butter until it gathered, and then she brought it dripping into the bowl, where she wielded a wooden paddle until every bit of milk was worked out. Then she pressed the mass into a wooden mold and set it covered just outside the door. In a few moments it could be pressed out into the milk-glass butter dish, and upon its golden surface would be molded a lovely maple leaf. They always ate around the leaf as long as possible. Zeke vowed it was much too "purty" to eat.

Kitty saw Zeke come limping into the barnyard. He was tying a rope to the barn door, meaning to attach it to the back door of the house. Kitty knew by this that he anticipated a heavy snowfall. He often took this measure in order to find the barn after a blizzard.

"There grew an old apple tree over his head, over his head," sang Kitty, discontinuing the butter molding long enough to hold her hands high over her head to show the children where the apple tree should grow. "O-o-h," chortled baby Sue. This shocked Chappy very much because it wasn't time to join in—not yet.

Kitty started to set the table; Zeke would be starved.

"Muthy, has you any food for m' cows? Just listen to 'em call—moo, moo-o-o, moo-o-o-o!" Chappy pushed buckeyes around the enclosure, and they mooed vicariously. Baby Sue's eyes grew round with interest, and she held her squash dolly to the edge of the bed to view the mooing cows.

Kitty's heart swelled within her—what darlings they were! And poor crippled, faithful Zeke—what a good father he was, out there puttering about the barn, anxiously preparing every protection for the comfort of the animals through the threatening storm.

At length he entered, bringing with him a whiff and tang of the outdoor frosty smell.

"Big snow due, Mamma!" he said, sniffing appreciatively at the fragrant supper. "Fe, fie, fo, fum, I smell goodies for my tum-tum," improvised Zeke as he gave the roller towel a twirl.

Chappy began to jump up and down in a sort of war dance: "Guess what we got for supper!"

Zeke glanced at the mush browning in the spider* upon the coals, "Shucks! It's just cawn meal with little bugs in it."

Chappy's face fell in disappointment: "Ah, Daddy, them's not bugs, them's sage and cracklins." Whereupon Daddy caught him up and tossed him high overhead, while Sue shrieked in sympathy.

The early winter dusk made it necessary to eat by lamplight. Kitty set the glass lamp, with its red flannel wick tinting the oil, in the center of the table, and by and by the first flakes of

---

* A cast-iron frying pan on a three-legged stand.

the threatened snow began to pat soft, feathery dabs upon the windowpane. The rising wind "whoo-ed" down the fireplace, sucking the flame upward, now outward. A sense of well-being possessed Zeke and Kitty. What if a storm roared without? There was plenty of wood, an abundance of homely fare, and they had their health and were together.

After the meal was dispatched and Julia Ann's gourd face bedaubed with sorghum in Sue's attempt to feed her, Kitty rose and cleared the table. Now came the most wonderful part of the day. Kitty went to the highboy in the corner and brought out the huge silver-clasped Bible. It had been their most treasured possession, a wedding gift, and was truly impressive, with deeply embossed covers and beautiful Doré illustrations. Zeke read a chapter every night, and tonight Chappy knelt upon a rush-bottomed chair, and Zeke gathered Sue and the ubiquitous Julia Ann into his lap, and turned the pages marked by the fringed ribbon that Kitty had embroidered in lilies.

First the children must see the colored pages that preceded the "Word"—here were the marriages, the births and deaths, gilt embossed. Sue's fat little finger pointed to the lettering that she knew by hearsay was her own. "Wead," she commanded, and Zeke read: "Elizabeth Susan Glenn, born June 6, 18— Now I wonder who on earth *that* could be?"

Zeke seemed puzzled, and Sue's cheeks were ruddy with excitement as she shrieked: "Me, me, that's *me!*" Zeke asked earnestly, "Is that a *fact?* Well, then, this name above it is maybe Chappy's. Yes, sir, if 'taint Chapman Edward Glenn. Well, bless my soul and body!"

"Turn to you, Muthy, Daddy, quick, cause Muthy's almost done with the dishes."

He turned to the ornately colored page besprinkled with doves, roses, and cupids, and within a golden wedding ring stood a picture of Dad and Muthy. True, the slim, black-coated groom didn't look much like poor lame Zeke, nor did the beveiled girl look at all like Kitty, but 'twas—for right there it said plain as anything, "Ezekiel W. Glenn to Katherine B. Spaulding."

Kitty had cleaned the three-legged pot and set it to dry before the fire; so Chappy knew that the time was growing short. He clamored for just one look at some of his "most favorite pitchures" before the chapter began. Zeke turned to the picture of the deluge, and Chappy's face grew sober as he looked at the huge tiger upon the water-surrounded knoll. He wondered if the mamma tiger was hurting her little kitten as she held it in her mouth away from the swirling waters.

Then there was the picture of a little boy carrying a bundle of sticks with which his father was to make a sacrificial fire for him. Oh—*to cook your own little boy!*

Muthy came with her basket of darning, and the fun was over. Chappy's attention wandered back to his livestock, and Zeke shifted the drowsy Sue to his left knee and solemnly began reading.

Outside the snow was now coming down in a thick white blanket; the wind blew about the little shelter, shaking the windows and sifting powdery ridges just inside the rudely built sills. Suddenly from without there came a long-drawn-out "Hello-oo!" and then "Zeke! Zeke!"

Zeke passed the baby to her mother, and went to the door. Peering out, he beheld the form of a man on a mule. The man had reined his mount to the side of the unporched doorway, and Zeke could see that it was old Mr. Witherspoon from across the bluff.

"Howdy, Mr. Witherspoon. 'Light and come in."

"Zeke, bundle up your folks and try to make it to the fort—Price's raiders are on their way here. They're raiding and burning and murdering—they're crazy with hunger and suffering, and they'll stop at nothing. Haste ye, Zeke—I'm on my way down the valley to warn the rest," and the old man spurred his mule through the storm, an old and travestied Paul Revere.

Zeke closed the door and turned to meet Kitty's terror-stricken eyes above the sleeping child's head. Little Chappy was playing un-concernedly at his barnyard. Zeke's heart contracted in an agony of fear—he knew they could never make it to the fort; his horse was slow, and the way was full of perils in such a storm. He could never find the trail, and they might wander about, only to die from exposure. But to stay meant to be murdered—burned alive.

Kitty's eyes were anxiously looking to him for a solution. His children were his to protect, to save. What, oh, what must he do? His distracted gaze fell upon a text in the open Bible: "He that dwelleth in the secret place of the Most High—" Zeke read it subconsciously, but with his ears tuned to the high shrieking of the wind.

"Put the babies to bed, Mamma, and cover them with everything in the house. I'm going to put out the fire. Hurry, darling."

Kitty's face was drawn and colorless, but there was a look of perfect trust as she set about complying.

Removing only the shoes of the children, she put them beneath the covers of the fat feather bed, gathering rugs, shawls, and coats to add to this.

"Why ain't you skinning me of my shirty an' things, Muthy?" Chappy was wide awake and curious about this strange procedure.

"Promise Muthy, darling boy, that you will be very, very quiet and try to sleep."

"Mustn't I even cough?"

"Try not to, Chappy."

"What if I sneeze?"

"Sh-hh!" tucking him in tightly.

Zeke was at the fireplace, pouring salt from a stone jar upon the flames. He drew the blinds of both windows to the sills, motioned Kitty to wrap herself in a blanket, and then put out the lamp.

He took Kitty's hand, and drew her gently to the side of the bed. Together they knelt, and Zeke whispered an earnest prayer for protection. He called upon the Lord for fulfillment of the precious promises in which he so devoutly believed: "I will lift up mine eyes unto the hills, from whence cometh my help. My help cometh from the Lord, which made heaven and earth."

Kitty smothered her sobs in the bedcovers while Zeke's earnest voice pleaded on: "He will not suffer thy foot to be removed: He that keepeth thee shall not slumber."

Far, far down the road there rose a clamor; hoarse shouts could be heard, and Kitty drew to Zeke's side, trembling violently. His strong arm crept about her, but he prayed on without faltering.

At a slit of the drawn blind there seeped in a rosy flare; it flickered and flared, growing brighter, and then it dimmed. Zeke swallowed hard. That would be old man Witherspoon's home. Gone—ashes now. Poor old man had wasted precious moments to warn Zeke. Zeke sent up a soundless prayer for this good neighbor.

Now they could hear the sound of horses' hoofs slashing through the snow, their bodies bumping against one another in the snow and darkness. Shouts of crazed men as they goaded their mounts, rang out. They must be as close as the west meadow—soon they would come into view of the house.

Baby Sue murmured in her sleep. Her little fat arms drew from beneath the cover. "Julia Ann—eat 'lasses." she murmured. Kitty captured the restless hand in the darkness and restored it to the warmth of the quilts. A haze of stark, acute anxiety gripped at her heart. It wouldn't be so terrible to die herself—but the *children*. Incapable of praying herself, she strained her ears for Zeke's whispered words which did not falter: "He who smiteth the rock for water in the desert, He who parteth a path in the midst of the sea—surely Thou canst raise a wall to protect and save these Thy children who trust in Thee."

Then reverently Zeke thanked God that he had heard his prayer, while closer and closer to the little house came the maddened raiders. Firebrands glanced here and there, and hoarse shouts and exultant cries rang out. Now and again snatches of war song parodies were heard, the rattle of a trace chain was heard. The torches seemed to penetrate the room, to creep beneath the very lids of Kitty's closed eyes. But no, it was only her fevered imagination—the flickering of a chimera.

Time seemed to halt in its tracks. Had they seen the house? Were they even now coming up the lane? Were they creeping up to break in or fire the roof? It seemed to the gentle parents kneeling in prayer by their babies that eons had passed since they had first knelt there. A stupor seemed to beset Kitty; in a daze she felt Zeke's hand tighten on hers. *Now* it had come— But, no, Zeke wouldn't like her to think this— "O thou of little faith," she chided her numb brain.

Hours seemed to have passed, and then Zeke leaned over and whispered in her ear: "Darling, I believe they have passed. Listen: doesn't it seem as if the sound is growing faint?"

A long time they listened, scarcely daring to breathe, hardly daring to hope. Fainter and fainter grew the shouts, the ribald songs, the rattle of chains, and still Zeke kept to his knees, praying and praising and thanking God for fulfillment.

Worn out with emotion, Kitty drowsed. The room grew bitter cold. The rose geranium, touched by the chill, curled its scalloped, fragrant leaves and died. A frosty vapor rose from Zeke's still moving lips. Tired, Kitty slept with her head upon the warm, breathing bodies of her babies.

After a time Zeke slept, only to be awakened by a slit of gray light that showed be-neath the drawn blinds. Why! 'Twas daylight. Zeke strained his ears. A perfect silence pervaded. There was no sound save the gnawing of a hungry mouse in the rafters. He ventured from his stiff posture, gained his feet, and crept cautiously to the window. Day was breaking fast. Behind clouds a fickle sun was making ready to shine upon a world so lately wracked with wind and snow. The bitter force of the wind had died to a sibilant whisper. All seemed calm and serene, and there was no mark on the placid scene that told of last night's savage raiding. Nature had sifted a cleansing covering over the ravage of fire.

Zeke cautiously lifted a portion of the blind, and the dazzle of the snow hurt his eyes. He stood shivering and blinking. Somehow it seemed an alien scene. His sleep-numbed brain suddenly functioned, and he now saw through the frosted pane something that thrilled his heart with a reverential awe. He ran the blind to the top of the window. Regardless of the sleeping babies, his voice rang out clarion clear with exultation: "Kitty! Kitty! Mamma, come—awake, darling! and see the wondrous miracle that God hath wrought!"

Kitty stumbled from her cramped posture and staggered to Zeke's side. He caught her in his arms, and his trembling forefinger pointed through the little window that faced the roadway, and there Kitty's wide, awed eyes beheld a wall of glistening snow, blown by the wind into a drift higher than their house—a wall that hid their abode from the eyes of the raiders and from their searching torches as they passed last night!

Once more Kitty and Zeke dropped to their knees and bowed their heads in thanksgiving: "He shall cover thee with His feathers, and under His wings shalt thou trust."

Grandmother Glenn stirred and sat erect. Where was Zeke now? The room was so cold, the fire must be rekindled before she could dress Chappy and Sue. Her rose geranium had frozen—she had forgotten to cover it after all. What happiness, though, that they were safe! Had all their other good neighbors been wiped out? Where was Zeke? Why didn't he come and help her with the babies?

Grandmother's eyes fell upon her gnarled, veiny hands. With a shock she came back to the present. Zeke was dead. Well, no matter, it wouldn't be long now—she was old. These hands—hands that had been so soft and plump— Voices floated to her from the living room. Sue's voice—Sue was a grown woman. Why, Zeke, our little Sue has a child of her own, little Bee. But no, even Bee wasn't little any more. My, but it seemed such a short time ago that Sue had played with Julia Ann, the squash dolly. She listened to Sue's words:

"—and *that*, Bee, is the story of white walls that Father told us so many times."

Why—why, after all, Grandmother hadn't been dreaming or reminiscing; she had been listening to Sue tell the well-known tale to Bee.

The insistent ring of the phone broke a throbbing silence, and Grandmother heard Bee's voice answering it, and then a rush of steps as Bee threw her arms around her mother's shoulders, half laughing, half crying.

"Mother, Mother! I feel like a dog—I don't deserve it! But listen, you'll never guess—prayers *are* answered! I mean your prayers for worthless me. Grandfather's miracle has repeated itself. Now listen carefully, darling: that was the Ohio Board of Hospitals, and they said that on the recommendation of the St. Matthew's faculty heads, I have been chosen to broadcast their health talks—little home facts about everyday precautions that everyone should know and so few do. It will mean a big fat contract at a salary that will floor you! And now Grandmother Glenn will have all her comforts and any more that you can think of, Mother. I feel so unworthy. Do you know, I'm going to ask to be announced as The Voice."

"The Voice, darling?"

"Yes!" exultantly. "The Voice from the white walls!" 🌿

*H*ave you ever seen someone approach you whose face is terribly disfigured or grotesque? What do you say? What do you think? Do you ever think, What if that were me?

God never rejects us—but we often reject Him, turn Him away. As happens in this story. Until . . .

If It Be God's Will

Phyllis Jeanne Branard

For today is life," reads a Sanskrit quotation, and Ellen Marshall has come to realize just how significant one day in a person's life can be, because in the space of a few hours on two memorable days she became the most miserable and the most wonderfully blest girl in her hometown.

Sitting in seventh-grade English class one day, Ellen smiled at her friend Kathy, who sat across the aisle, and suddenly felt her mouth twitch convulsively. Kathy's answering smile was transformed into one of incredulity, then of horror, and she whispered, "Your mouth!"

Ellen sensed that something indescribable and terrible was happening to her face. What? she wondered. In a matter of seconds her face began to feel numb and grotesque.

In the discussion that followed, Ellen tried to put thoughts of herself out of mind and concentrate on what the teacher was saying, but her face felt so strange. Her head had developed a throbbing pain, she was dizzy, and it was difficult to think straight.

Finally the bell rang for separation of classes, and Ellen hurried to geography, where she was to give an oral report. If only she could get through this one class, then she could go home.

The teacher called for Ellen to give her report. She got up, walked to the front of the room, and began, but the voice that came from her mouth was not hers. The words were indistinct and difficult to form; such sounds as *f, p, b, m,* and *v* sounded fuzzy. Her head was spinning now, and when she heard a snicker from the class she realized that she was pointing to cities on the blackboard instead of on the map. The map was about two feet from where she was standing.

Sensing something was wrong, the teacher asked, "What's the matter, Ellen?" Ellen staggered toward a chair.

"I don't feel so well," she said.

Kathy, Ellen's best friend, walked home with her that afternoon and left her lying on the couch in the living room. It was there that

Ellen's mother found her when she came in at four-thirty from a shopping trip. Mrs. Marshall saw her thirteen-year-old daughter pitching feverishly, the youthful face ugly and contorted when she tried to speak. Mrs. Marshall felt a pang of fear.

The next morning Ellen and her mother went to see the family doctor. His face was a passionless mask as his sensitive fingers examined the left side of the distorted face. He was silent, pensive. Then he said, "Mrs. Marshall, there is nothing I can do for your daughter. She has a severe case of facial paralysis, and I'm not a specialist in that field. I could, perhaps, treat her, but I would rather turn the case over to Dr. Briston. He is a reliable doctor, young and capable—one in whom you can put complete trust. I'll phone and tell him you're coming."

Dr. Briston smiled warmly as they entered his office. He was a tall man—a bit too thin, Mrs. Marshall thought, but rather nice looking in a plain, clean-cut way. His voice was soothing and assuring.

He motioned for Ellen to sit down. "Now, let's see, young lady, what seems to be the trouble?" Ellen tried to smile, but it was such a self-conscious effort, with one side smiling and the other not, that she gave up.

Dr. Briston was thoughtful as he repeated the half-pinching of her left jaw. Then he told Mrs. Marshall, in terms she could understand, that her daughter was paralyzed on the left side of her face, and that it sometimes took a long time to cure. Some patients recovered within a few months, he said; some within a year, but for some it took many years. He did not know how long it would take Ellen, but he would do his best.

Mrs. Marshall was sick at heart. Her lovely young daughter stricken with paralysis! How Ellen must feel—so youthful and vivacious—to be robbed overnight of girlhood's normal pleasures! How would her sensitive nature respond to this sudden calamity?

At the dinner table Ellen was painfully aware of the suppressed grins on her brothers' faces. Both Dan and Charles realized their sister had a serious malady, but try as they might, it was next to impossible to refrain from smiling. Pixie, as they affectionately called her, could not eat without holding her mouth open with the fingers on her left hand as she pushed the food in bite by bite.

Ellen went upstairs and dressed for bed. The doctor had said she could go to school, but she did not want her friends to see her this way. She could not face their pitying glances. She would not go! Defiantly she stared at her image in the mirror. Bitter eyes looked out at her; a twisted, ugly mouth smiled sourly on one side while the other side remained solemn. She wrinkled her forehead; one side remained smooth.

"You ugly old witch!" she burst out suddenly. "Ugly, ugly, ugly!" She repeated the words and flung herself across the bed, her body shaking with sobs. "Why, Lord? Why?"

Sleep came slowly and then was troubled with dreams of hands pointing accusingly at her face, cruel, misshapen mouths smirking at her. She saw a witch with *her* face who kept repeating, "Mirror, mirror on the wall, who is fairest of them all?"

Ellen awoke in a cold sweat.

The next three weeks dragged by. Ellen went out only to the doctor's office. Her brothers brought her magazines, which she read from cover to cover until her eyes were so tired she could not hold them open. Then she slept.

Each night she stared at the strange creature in the mirror until the practice held an ominous fascination for her. She wondered whether she would ever be cured. Others had had this affliction for years. Could she hope to have God cure her and not the others?

Mr. and Mrs. Marshall were devout Christians and believed in the healing powers of an omnipotent God. As soon as Ellen became stricken they told the members of the small Bridgeville church and asked for special remembrance of Ellen in prayer. At all religious meetings during the weeks that followed Ellen's case was petitioned to God, and one meeting was canceled in order that the group might have special prayer for their little pixie. Everyone loved Ellen and had believed she would do great things for the Lord someday. Why, then, this great disaster? It was not their right to question, but to pray.

Ellen's faith was failing her little by little. She had abandoned prayer, for what good did it do? Would God heal her when He had not healed similar cases?

It was Wednesday night, three weeks after that fatal day in class. Ellen was sitting in her room looking at the pictures in a fashion magazine. Reading was her sole pleasure now—through magazines she was able to forget herself. Lately, she had read everything she could get her hands on, though she knew her mother would not have approved had she seen some of the stories.

Ellen put the magazine down. Her head ached. On the stairway footsteps sounded, and in a few minutes Mr. Marshall appeared at the doorway. His dark eyes looked tired.

"I brought you a book," he said. Ellen wondered what it would be. She knew all too well her father's taste in literature. His bookshelves were full of Chinese history, meteorology, philosophy, and textbooks on mathematics and grammar.

She held the book gingerly in her lap. It was something about physiology. Her father had placed a bookmark at the beginning of a chapter discussing prayer.

Ellen leafed through the pages and caught herself reading snatches of the book. The style of the author was a little deep, but she could understand most of what he was saying. One statement about the mental factor in a person's case was very significant. He said you had to believe you were going to get well, or you never would. You had to expect it.

Time has a way of slipping by, and before Ellen realized, it was so late that Mother was home from prayer meeting. She came in to see whether there was anything Ellen wanted before she went to bed.

"Ellen," her mother asked rather unexpectedly, "do you ever pray that you will be healed?"

Ellen shook her head no. "What's the use?" she asked. "I'm paralyzed, and I might just as well get used to the fact."

"Listen to me for a minute, Ellen. All the people in the church have been praying for you, your father and brothers have prayed for you, and I've prayed for you. But if you don't have enough desire to get well to pray for yourself, then I'm afraid our prayers won't do much good."

There was more. Ellen and Mrs. Marshall talked until ten-thirty, and finally Ellen promised to pray. What her mother said had impressed her deeply.

Ellen put on her pajamas, took her Bible off the bedstand, and began to read. She read in the New Testament of the healing Christ had performed while on earth. It gave her comfort and hope. Her father's book came into her mind, as did the things her mother had said. Finally, she threw herself across the bed and wept bitterly.

That night she rededicated her life to Christ and prayed earnestly and promised that if it was God's will to heal her, she would leave junior high school and attend a Christian academy. She wanted to have a part in the finishing of His work in the earth.

Ellen awoke late the next morning. The sun was streaming in through the window, and in a nearby tree a robin twittered cheerfully. She was rested and felt that it was good to be alive. A thought flashed through her mind: *Whistle.* She puckered her lips, and a soft sharp sound came out. Not able to believe her ears, she repeated the performance. *She could whistle!* Excitedly she went to the mirror and wrinkled her forehead, winked her left eye, and then smiled! *She was healed!*

Ellen flew down the stairway and into the kitchen, where her mother was cooking breakfast.

"Mom! Mom!" she cried. "Look!" Then she went through the whole process of wrinkling her forehead, winking, and smiling broadly. Mrs. Marshall was so excited she dropped one of her favorite teacups and broke it. But of what significance is a teacup when your daughter is healed!

Both were eager to show Dr. Briston the marvelous recovery. He was just as excited as they were, and dismissed them from his office in a few minutes with a friendly, "Guess you don't need me anymore."

True to her word, Ellen went to an acad-emy, paying her tuition by doing housework. Always she witnessed for the divine Healer who had wrought a miracle for her. After graduation she enrolled in a Christian college where her two brothers are also students. In a few years Ellen will be able to go out into the work of God as a church school teacher.

Does God hear and answer prayer? Ellen Marshall's life is an affirmative answer to, and a living example of, this great truth. ❧

*A*nd just to think of the odds without a cell phone!

Teresa A. Sales

Dear Lord, please don't let that black cloud of smoke be coming from our car!" I pleaded. Unfortunately, our immediate loss of power told me that the noxious cloud was, indeed, the dying gasps of our small vehicle.

It was late summer 2001, and we were headed to Denver to catch a plane for a month-long budget tour of eleven European countries, the culmination of years of dreaming and months of saving.

We had left Pueblo early, so we could enjoy a leisurely lunch with our two Denver daughters before going to the airport for the long flight to London. Unfortunately, we did not have a cell phone at that time, and we were five miles from Castle Rock, the nearest town. I contemplated with dismay how long it would take to walk to the nearest phone to get help.

Our car slowly rolled to the shoulder of I-25 and stopped right behind the only car we had seen on the side of the highway the entire trip. If anything, this abandoned vehicle appeared to be in worse shape than ours!

I bowed my head and immediately sent up a quick appeal to Heaven: "Lord, send us an angel!" I knew it would take a miracle for anyone to stop on that busy interstate and help a stranded motorist.

As I opened my eyes, an antiquated tow truck, about as pathetic as the old car it had come to retrieve, stopped in front of the two deceased cars. Two African-American men—one older and shorter, the other younger and taller—climbed out of the truck to determine how to hook up the car ahead of us for towing. The men wore faded mechanics' shirts with logos on them. The shirts and their logos were from two different auto-repair businesses, and the logo on the truck was different from those worn by the men.

I jumped out of our still-smoking car and ran over to the men. "Does either of you have a cell phone?" I queried. "Our motor has just burned up, and we need to call for help—we have a plane to catch!" The younger man nodded and handed me a phone, then went about the business of hooking up the auto they had come to remove.

I called our youngest daughter, who lives at Highlands Ranch, twenty miles from where our car had abandoned us, and she told us that although her husband was scheduled to be north of Denver that day inspecting some new homes in which his company was installing heating and air conditioning, he had gotten a call to be in the Castle Rock area instead, and was very close to the place where we sat stranded. Another answer to prayer!

I gratefully took the cell phone back to the young man and thanked him profusely for allowing us to use it. He spoke for the first time. "We would be glad to tow you in, but we can only take one car at a time, and we have a ways to go."

"We're fine now, thanks to you," I said. "Your timing was perfect!"

Then I turned to the older man and said emotionally, "You are angels!" He smiled, nodded his head affirmatively, and softly said, "Yes," as he walked to the tow truck and drove away.

Our son-in-law rescued us shortly, transferred our luggage to his truck, and arranged for a tow truck to take our car into Castle Rock. We made our plane, and we've never forgotten how our prayer for help that day fourteen years ago was answered instantly, just as Daniel's angel arrived with help as he finished praying. ❧

SECTION TWO

"But each day the Lord pours his unfailing love upon me, and through each night I sing his songs, praying to God who gives me life."
—Psalm 42:8, NLT

"We tend to place God's activity in a different category from natural or human activity; the Bible tends to draw them together. Somehow God works in all of creation, all of history, to bring about ultimate goals."
—Yancey, page 139

*S*ince I am twice a Leininger (my maternal grandmother and grandfather were cousins, so my grandmother didn't even have to change her name when they married), I've always been captivated by Leininger history. Consequently, when I stumbled on the story of the abduction of two of my ancestors by Shawnee and Delaware Indians, I didn't rest until I had cobbled together the whole gripping narrative, which was first articulated by Henry M. Muhlenberg (1711–1787), founder of the Lutheran Church in America. In reconstructing the story, I was assisted by Regina Leininger and Maria LeRoy.

Hymns as prayers and prayers as hymns—the essence of this story.

ALONE, YET NOT ALONE AM I

Henry Melchior Muhlenberg
with Regina Leininger and Maria LeRoy

"Sing for us, mutter," pleaded Regina, as the sycamore and pine crackled and flared against the back log in the rough stone fireplace of the lonely cabin.

"Ach, kinder, what shall I sing to you—a Schlaflied?"

She was a broad, strong woman, ruddy and handsome, with the buxom vigor that belonged to her hale German heredity and her life in the wilderness of the strange new world. Beside the rough pine table, her husband used the evening's hearth light to repair a crude piece of harness. Around her were her children: two sons and as many daughters. The boys were in their teens, but self-reliant, with the air of pioneer boys who have already learned their lessons of woodcraft. The girls were children still. Regina was not yet ten years old, and Barbara, her sister, whose hand she held as she spoke, was only twelve.

Odd hands they were. Their thumbs were already flattened to a marked spatula by the twisting of flax that filled every spare instant of their waking hours, except for this last interlude before they should bundle into the shut-in bunk that had been called a bed in Germany. Their mother had just such a hand marked with just such a thumb, grossly exaggerated. Hers had been acquired across the sea and must remain deformed until she died.

The hides drying on the cabin walls, and the skins comprising some of the garments of the boys and their father, were evidence of the substitutes these pioneers used for wool in this new country, where sheep were the easy prey of wolf and panther. . . .

But good linen the careful German housewife must have, and her daughters were growing up to the domestic virtues under expert guidance. . . . Men, in those times, looked at a girl's thumb for just such an unnatural flattening.

Regina, who was the pet of the family, pondered her mother's suggestion for a minute.

"Oh mutter," she said, "sing what thou

dost always sing—'Allein, Doch Nich Allein Ein Ich.' "

Her clear, blue eyes on the flames and her full maternal bosom swelling as she took the higher notes of the old hymn, the pioneer's wife intoned with the girls adding low their sweet sopranos and the boys humming to their father's rumbling bass:

Alone, yet not alone am I,
Though in this solitude so drear,
I feel my Savior always nigh;
He comes the weary hours to cheer,
I am with Him, and He with me—
E'en here alone I cannot be.

She sang the hymn through, and a blessed peace seemed to fill the tiny cabin, its door made fast by the great crossbar of oak, its one window shuttered with a two-inch plank, barred too.

"Bed now, kinder!" she commanded. "I must go to the mill in the morning."

But Regina pleaded, as a child will, "Ach, mutter, the fire isn't dead yet. Sing again. Let's sing 'Jesus, Evermore I Love.' "

So the mother sang that hymn too. And again the family joined their voices to hers in the music that was a prayer—a prayer, like the first, of the kind whose need none knew better than these adventurers into a region that only the most needy and the most daring penetrated.

"Nun, schneil!" she cried briskly. "Come, vater"—to her husband—"put it aside. It is early morning tomorrow."

Leininger . . . hung his scrap of harness on a nail. The embers flickered and fell away against the back log. The wilderness, with its one small group of human beings, sank into its quiet slumber, prelude to one of the goriest Indian massacres Pennsylvania's border history ever knew.

We pride ourselves now on our fair treatment of our early savages. But the traditions of the tribes carried long and bitter grudges born of the white man's double dealing and treachery, and the day Frau Leininger had appointed for riding with the grist to the mill was the day the red man had chosen for a bloody reckoning.

The Leiningers' home was near the present town of Selinsgrove, on the edge of the line run by the English as the boundary of the land they had acquired from the Six Nations by the Albany Treaty of July 6, 1754. The boundary lay about a mile from the juncture of Penn's Creek with the Susquehanna River. In August of 1754, the Delaware Indians, at a conference they had demanded, denounced the treaty on the ground that under the tribal agreement, the Six Nations had no right to give away that territory without the consent of the Delawares. The English paid no heed to the protest, but went ahead and sold settlers rights to a score and more families. Before the autumn was past, the Leiningers and their fellow pioneers had made their homes along Penn's Creek. They were Europe's furthest outposts in its relentless seizure of a continent.

Braddock's defeat meant the Indians' chance to recover their own. The Delawares cast their lot with the French, whose campaign required immediate control of the ground where the two branches of the Susquehanna join at Sunbury. Adjoining the territory, owned by the Delawares, it would give them control of the approaches and operations against eastern and southern Pennsylvania.

The English countered by erecting Fort Augusta, which held the French at bay. But the Indians, fiercely resentful of the wrongs done them, carried on the invasion along their own sudden, sanguine lines of campaign. The tale of their first unheralded onslaught, the brunt of which was born by the hapless pioneers along Penn's Creek, long thrilled fireside groups with horror. . . .

When the Leiningers rose on the morning of October 16, 1755, a year after they'd built their cabin in the wilderness, they guessed nothing of the impending disaster. For all the presence of other settlers in the region, the solitude about them seemed absolute. A couple of dozen cabins scattered over the leagues

might have been so many birds' nests.

Breakfast, substantial as the German pioneers liked it and the game-filled land provided, delayed the careful housewife's departure. She must be sure that Barbara and Regina would wash all the dishes well; that they would ready the house while she was away; that they knew what to prepare for dinner should she be delayed in her return. One of the boys must go with her; the other could stay at home helping his father. At last all her routine was arranged.

"Good-bye!" she called cheerfully as she and her boy struck into the path through the forest.

Some miles away, in even more leisurely fashion, fast had been broken around their campfires by the hundreds of grim Delawares, with the Shawnees, their allies. The warriors made even more elaborate toilettes, adding touches of their war paint until an unearthly hideousness distorted the pitiless hawk look of their dusky features.

Their tomahawks in hand, every one fitting accurately his tread into the steps of the others, they sped naked and shadowlike toward Penn's Creek.

The series of surprises was complete. Like the Leiningers, none of the settlers suspected their doom until it leaped, with blood-curdling war whoops, upon them. Leininger and his son, each seized by a couple of savages, were tomahawked and scalped in the clearing of their little cabin while the girls stared, shrieking from where they stood in the midst of their household tasks. In a space no longer than a minute, the two sisters, from happiness and freedom, were transformed into captives and slaves.

Just as they were, Barbara and Regina were bound and dragged into the forest by the Indians, their last glance back at their home telling them that it was in flames. As they progressed, they described pillars of smoke, the burning homes of their neighbors.

After a while their captors halted, flinging them to the ground. Then, leaving several braves to guard them, the others sped away to fresh slaughter.

From time to time Indians arrived, dragging more captives to the rendezvous. Soon the sisters realized what must be the extent and also the appalling nature of the massacre. It was deadly ominous that among all the prisoners there were only children, many of them babies scarcely able to walk. Most of them were girls, and where boys had been spared, they were very young. Women and men—all who were past the age at which the Indians believed them capable of complete absorption into the tribal life—had been ruthlessly tomahawked and scalped.

Several days passed, while the sisters, in company of the ever-increasing number of child prisoners, remained under guard, and the country for miles around was laid waste with fire and tomahawk. Braves carried in terrified children, whose faces were bloodstained from the scalps of their mothers, hanging from their captors' belts. At first, throughout this frightened multitude of children, a low whimpering prevailed. But the blows that were sure to fall on anyone who murmured ere long reduced them to a frightened stillness, and they lay or sat, horror-eyed, while their bodies began to waste from the hunger they endured throughout their waiting.

At length, when all the Indians concerned in the massacre had assembled with their child prisoners, the trail was taken up towards the lands of the Delawares and the Shawnees. Barbara and Regina, like the other girls whose years and strength made it possible for them to carry burdens, were given little ones to carry on their backs, where the babies were strapped securely.

Steadily westward for hundreds of miles that terrible trail was followed. From the start, any line of progress that bore a resemblance of a pathway was avoided. The Indians were only too aware that once word of their raid was spread, pursuit would be instant. They were making it as dubious and difficult as possible.

The tramping children were all barefoot, yet unused to such rough traveling. The way led through mire and swamps, among the underbrush and briars, over brush and sharp flint. Yet not for a moment did the savages check the speed of their retreat. The girl who fell with her burden was whipped on like a tired pony. Those tender feet were soon cut and torn to the very bones, and the tendons in some were severed. Scarcely a day had gone by before the clothes in which they had been captured were torn from their shoulders by the underbrush; they made the rest of their awful journey as naked as the Indians themselves.

After many days of such anguish, the Indians began to make frequent halts, at which some child would drop out of line to be turned over to a woman in an Indian village they had reached. Their captors were complying with the tribal rule that where parents had lost any of their children in warfare, they must be recompensed with captives, henceforth their slaves, with adoption into the tribe as their sole hope of mitigating the misery of their lot.

"Barbara," whispered Regina to her sister, "will they leave one of us in one place and carry the other further on?"

"I'm afraid so," Barbara replied.

"Oh, I don't know what I shall do if I am left all alone!" And the younger sister began to cry.

"I don't know either," said Barbara. "I

only hope they send thee away first. Thou wilt then be so much the nearer home. Maybe thou canst escape sometime, when thou art older."

Regina shuddered.

"I can never escape," she wept. "We are so far away now that I couldn't go back if they sent me."

Still the sisters were driven onward, in company with the slowly diminishing line of captives. It was not until many days more—naked, barefoot, laden each with her appointed burden of younger childhood—that the fateful halt came at the village that was to claim one of them. There was no warning; no preparation. Regina was shoved, the child strapped to her back, into the hut of an ill-favored old hag, of whose children only one son, a notorious village loafer, survived.

"Barbara!" Regina she screamed in her despair. She heard her sister's voice call a hopeless farewell, on her back the two-year-old child she had carried the distance of four hundred miles, as she was driven westward beyond Regina's vision. The older girl bore the murderous fatigues of that journey for another hundred miles before she found her place of slavery in the territory now comprised within the sovereign state of Ohio.

For three and a half years Barbara Leininger served her Indian mistress there as a slave, her one solace the friendship of a girl captive near her age, Maria LeRoy. The girls gradually were given some slight measure of freedom, for their owners deemed it out of all likelihood that anyone, man or woman, should ever dare the risk of flight with so terrible a journey to follow before they could reach the English outpost. Yet, when the two young girls were just budding into womanhood and were liable to be forced into union with some young men of the tribe, that daring venture was agreed upon by Barbara with a young Englishman, David Breckenridge, who had attained manhood in captivity. She told Maria LeRoy. The season was February, and Maria, saying she was willing enough to risk it, advised that they wait until the weather should be milder.

But their resolve once taken, it was hard for any of the captives to endure their wretched situation. The lapse of a month found them eager to take whatever desperate chances the close of the winter offered, and another Englishman, Owen Gibson, was enlisted in the enterprise. At ten o'clock in the night of March 16, 1759, Owen, with the noiseless tread he had learned among the Indians, reached Barbara's little lean-to and gave her the faint signal for which she waited. David had in the meantime met Maria LeRoy, and the four made their way stealthily through the quiet village, in no dread of their masters, but in deadly fear of the sixteen dogs that lurked in the lee of the huts. By some blessed mercy of providence, not a cur barked.

Their flight, of course, was eastward, and their speed was the greatest they could make. After some traveling, breathless for the most part, they found themselves on the bank of the Muskingum River, too bitterly cold, too wide, and too deep to ford or swim.

When Barbara Leininger and her companions, hearkening for sounds of pursuit, stood on that fateful shore, their faces toward the land that meant life and happiness, they believed that God was there beside them and would answer their appeal if they would have faith in Him. Barbara, her face wearing the rapt expression of one inspired, called upon her memories of the hymns her mother sang, mingling into one softly intoned prayer the lines that might tell their God of the dire need they suffered.

As she finished, it seemed to all of them that the prayer must have been answered from on high. They found a raft fashioned by Indians and abandoned to the waters after it had served its purpose of ferriage across the Muskingum.

The current carried them a mile downstream before they could effect their landing on the opposite bank; but they were only too grateful both for their passage across that first daunting obstacle and for having put out of their pursuers' reach the raft that could have facilitated the pursuit.

All that night and all the next day they ran until utterly exhausted, and then they flung themselves on the cold ground without daring to kindle even the smallest campfire.

In the morning they awoke ravenous, and Owen was forced to risk on a bear the noise of a gunshot from the weapon he carried. The bear fell, and he ran to tomahawk it. But the bear, as the young Englishman closed in, caught his foot in its powerful jaws, inflicting three wounds that seriously lamed him, and then made its escape among the rocks. They then limped on their dangerous way, drawn with hunger pangs.

Another day passed and still no game. But on the third day Owen killed a deer, and the hind quarters, roasted, refreshed the whole party. Next morning another deer, falling to the same true aim, furnished food that carried them to the Ohio River, which they reached at night, having made a detour of one hundred miles to find it.

They slept until midnight. David and Owen rose then and built a raft on which the little party crossed. Learned enough in Indian lore to read the sign language, they found markings there that informed them that 150 miles still separated them from Fort Duquesne. But how the trail lay they could not surmise.

So they held a council of war, agreed that their only course was to travel straight onward toward the sunrise, and for seven days they retraced their way back through the wilderness until they reached Little Beaver Creek, fifty miles from Pittsburgh.

It seemed as though every misfortune they had successfully weathered must befall them almost within touch of safety. Barbara, slipping into a stream, nearly drowned. Owen lost his flint and steel, and amid rain and snow, they passed four days and nights without a glimmer of fire. On the last day of that eventful March they came to the river three miles below Pittsburgh. There they pushed off on a raft they had hastily flung together. It proved too small for their combined weight and began to sink under them. Maria LeRoy fell into the river and was saved only by the devotion of her companions. They returned to the bank, then the young men ferried them across the Monongahela one at a time.

Safe now, but unable in the dark to risk the frail craft in reaching the fort beyond, they called for aid. Colonel Hugh Mercer, in command, sent a boat; but the men in it, for a time believing the strangers were Indians, refused to take them in. It was almost impossible to persuade the soldiers that the two girls with their companions had made the appalling journey from the far land of the savages. But at length, when the shivering fugitives adduced fact after fact in support of their declaration, the boat's crew consented to forego the evidence of their eyes, took them aboard, and speedily landed them at the fort.

Once there and the salient features of their story known, they were given every help and comfort. Colonel Mercer ordered each of the girls provided with a new chemise, a petticoat, stockings, garters, and such other items as decency and warmth demanded. A day later he sent them forward under guard of a detachment of soldiers commanded by Lieutenant Samuel Miles to Fort Ligonier, where the lieutenant presented them with blankets. On April 15, under the protection of Captain Philip Weiser and Lieutenant Samuel J. Atlee, they were escorted to Fort Bedford, where they remained for a week. They found accommodation in wagons as far as Harris Ferry, and thence, afoot, they took their way to Lancaster and on to Philadelphia, where they were reunited with their families.

Meanwhile, through all those years, Barbara's young sister, Regina, had lived the true slave's life in the service of the hag to whom her captors had given her. The younger girl's evil augury that, though she might be nearer the settlements than her sister, she could never escape, was destined to be correct.

The old squaw's son was the true type of young Indian loafer and sport. He went away for days and weeks at a time and, for all he cared, left his mother to starve.

Regina, in her lowly status of slave girl, was given the alternative of providing food for the squalid household or of being put to death.

Naked, starving, the child gathered the wood that supplied warmth for the miserable shack of boughs in which they huddled. She dug in the fields and woods for roots, artichokes, garlic, and whatever might prove edible, not excepting the bark of some trees. When the ground froze, she hunted like a wild beast for field mice, wood rats, and other small animals that could stay the pangs of hunger.

As the years went by, the child she had carried into the village on her back grew big enough to be of some help in that desperate, unremitting struggle against starvation. Regina herself, her youthful vitality responding to the hardships of her existence, developed into magnificent young womanhood, tall and strong of frame, her body bronzed under the sunlight, her regular features making her a rarely beautiful Indian maiden.

Outwardly, she appeared reconciled to her fate. She spoke the tribal language, she lived the tribal life; from her memory the recollection of even her mother's face departed.

But in her heart she treasured her native tongue; and above all, she cherished the words of the hymns in which, in the cabin home on the cruel borderline, she had joined her childish treble to the strong inspiring volume of her mother's notes.

When, with her young companion, she found herself alone in the forest, drudging at the task of reaping where no one had sowed, Regina would kneel, and her heart welling with fond, unavailing memories, repeat the words of those hymns solemnly as her prayers for deliverance. As she neared womanhood there began to dawn in her soul a simple, trusting faith that some time in some way, how she knew not, the hour of her release from bondage must arrive.

She was almost nineteen years old when the bold campaign against the tribes pushed by Colonel Bouquet into their remotest fortresses beyond the Ohio compelled the savages to sue for peace.

"The first condition under which any mercy can be shown," he notified the beaten chiefs, "must be the immediate surrender into my keeping of every white prisoner held captive in every village of your tribes."

It was a strange and often shocking spectacle that followed during the ensuing weeks there in the trackless wilderness, while the victorious whites received from the savages hundreds of their race—men, women, and children—who had been mourned as dead or as forever lost by the few kin surviving the successive massacres.

In the midst of winter the poor creatures came, singly and in groups, well-nigh naked. The officers and the soldiers vied with one another in sacrificing portions of their uniforms, which could be used to supply some few of their charges with covering. As swiftly as marches could be made they conveyed the wretched throng to Fort Pitt. The garrison there emulated the men returning from the field. They gave up their capes, sleeves, pocket-flaps, pockets, collars, unneeded portions of their shirts, their cravats, extra blanket lengths—every smallest scrap of material that could be fashioned into extra clothing; and then, officers and men, they turned cutters and seamstresses and made the garments.

Word was now sent forward throughout Pennsylvania that the army of the rescued would be brought as far as Carlisle, where members of any family who had lost dear ones could come and claim their own, and the march to Carlisle followed.

History may afford no parallel for the mingling of the dramatic with the tragic that developed in the thrilling scene enacted in Carlisle on December 31, 1764, before English commissioners appointed to supervise the restoration of the captives to their families. All the prisoners of the Indians had not been spared to slavery as children. The varied fortunes of the recurring wars and raids had led the savages to carry off wives and husbands, as well as daughters and sons.

And there, on one hand an immense throng of whites, young and old, confronted a great crowd of brown-skinned people, who, where they were dressed at all, wore Joseph's coat of many colors or the wild scant garments of the Indians with whom they had to live so long. There were husbands who recognized instantly wives ravished from their homes. There were parents who could not recognize their own children. Laughter and tears, the extremes of joy and heart-breaking despair, met side by side amid those reunions and those failures of loved ones to find their own.

The journey to the grist mill on the cruel morning of the Penn's Creek massacre had saved Mrs. Leininger and her older boy from the fate of her younger son and her husband. She came to Carlisle, a woman changed and aged in her nine long years of grief, hoping passionately that her daughter Regina would be among the captives.

But now she stood, heart-wrung and sad-eyed, turning to the commissioners to implore their aid in identifying her. She told them, with a mother's fond words, of the Regina she had loved; of the little girl of ten, so

good and so gentle, whose pleasure was the singing of their homely German hymns.

"Do you remember the words of one of those hymns?" suddenly inquired a grave member of the official group.

"Ach, surely! She loved most the hymns 'Alone, Yet Not Alone Am I,' and 'Jesus, Evermore I Love.'"

"Why, then, step forth and sing it. It may be the child, no doubt a woman grown by this time, will recognize words or voice." Those nearest them noted, idly at the moment—for their own affairs were engrossing—a matron walking a few steps forward, where she might be free of the press of embraces and rejoicing surrounding her anguished suspense. Then, above the tumult, her face aglow with the longing of her mother love, and looking straight at the quivering group of captives still unclaimed, the mother of Regina Leininger raised her voice in the beautiful words of that old, sweet hymn of unfaltering faith: "Alone, yet not alone am I / Though in this solitude so dread—"

From the bronzed mass of humanity before her a tall, powerful girl, known only by her Indian name, Sawquehanna—the White Lily—sprang and ran forward. As she ran she sang: "I feel my Savior always nigh; / He comes the weary hours to cheer."

The mother's voice went on; in it there sounded a new note of sublime happiness, which, for once, took from their own joys and griefs the hearts of the hundreds who heard and saw; and although both felt at once that they were mother and child, their deep inbred religious sentiment so filled them with gratitude to the Most High that they stood, their arms outstretched in eagerness, yet waiting to clasp each other in an embrace until they finished the stanza together: "I am with Him and He with me, / E'en here alone I cannot be."

Then the mother bowed her graying head in silent prayer and drew to her bosom the child she had mourned so long.

"Ach, mutter, mutter!" cried Regina. "I remember them all. Listen! I must prove to thee again that I am thy little Regina."

She sang the rest of the hymn, and "Jesus, Evermore I Love." But as she began the second hymn, a brown little girl just growing into her teens ran from among the captives and, catching her hand, joined in the words. When Regina, immediately afterward recited the Apostles' Creed, the child repeated with her the solemn declaration of faith. She was the baby Regina had carried on her back into the hut of the old hag they were given to.

No one ever claimed the girl; but she, with every clinging tenderness of her child nature, claimed Regina. And so the mother, who had come hoping she might recover one daughter, returned to her home with two. ❧

*P*rior to credit cards (1960s), one either had money or one didn't. When one had no money, one could not even put food on the table for the family.

Today, even when they have no money, many people use credit cards. As a result, untold thousands of people have seen their indebtedness grow so great that they're forced to declare bankruptcy. Thus today, more and more such chastened people use debit cards instead of credit cards.

But this story speaks to us just as much today as it did back then.

How God Sent the Flour

Author Unknown

It was the hour for family worship. A dear old friend was visiting with Mother, so Bobby proudly handed her his new Bible to use. After worship was over, Mother's friend, Miss Clara, said to Bobby, "What a beautiful copy of God's Word you have!"

"Yes," answered Bobby, "it is the nicest Bible in the whole world, for God sent it right to me." Then he told her of his answer to prayer for a Bible of his very own.

"God always does above all we can ask or think," said Miss Clara. "He delights in 'going over the top' in good things."

"Did He ever supply your needs for something too?" asked Howard.

Miss Clara laughed and said, "That means you want a story." When she had cuddled up the baby and gathered the boys around her, she went on. "I'm going to tell you a true story of how God sent us food. When I was a girl, my father was a minister. Once when he had to go to the conference, he didn't have even one cent to leave Mother with which to buy food while he was gone. The people had not paid what they had promised. Father had just enough money to buy his ticket. He told Mother he would not go and leave us without money, but Mother quoted that beautiful verse that you have learned, 'My God shall supply all your need,' and told Father he must go, that God would take care of us.

"We had some potatoes, a few cans of fruit, a little dried corn, and salt and sugar in the house, but the flour bin was empty. Mother did not believe in going in debt, and we bought only what we could pay for. Oh, yes, I forgot to say that we still had one loaf of bread when Father left. But when that was gone, there was no flour to make any more. Mother smiled and told us that God knew we needed flour, so we shouldn't worry. She had us all kneel with her while she asked our heavenly Father to send us a sack of flour. When she arose, she made the rising for bread, just as if the flour bin were full. Then she said, 'Now children, I've done all I can; God will do the rest.' We all went to bed strong in faith that God would answer our prayers. I almost expected to wake up in the morning and find a sack of flour in the kitchen. When my brother came downstairs, the first thing he asked was, 'Has God sent the flour yet?'

"Mother lifted the lid from the bread bowl and let us see how light and foamy the rising was. All it needed was the flour. We ate our scant breakfast of potatoes and salt, and then Mother knelt by the empty flour bin and praised God because He had said His children would never need to beg for bread.

"Still no flour came. Mother and I washed the dishes, and Mother started to sing the old song, 'Oh, for a faith that will not shrink.' My little brother, who was looking out of the window, said, 'Somebody is tying a horse to our fence.' We children all hurried to look out, fully expecting to see the woman carry in some flour. To our great disappointment she came up the path empty-handed.

"Mother invited her in, and she sat down, acting rather embarrassed and strange. She was not a Christian and never had been to church, but her daughter had been converted during the revival Father had held; and I knew Father and Mother had been praying that she and her husband might know Jesus, too.

"She talked about the weather, and kept twisting her scarf. Finally she said, 'I want to tell you a strange thing that happened to me this morning. As I was getting breakfast, I heard a voice say, "Take Brother Hayden some flour." I knew no one was in the kitchen but me, and I got scared. Then I heard it again. "Go take Brother Hayden some flour." I suppose I'm a fool, but do you need flour?'

"By this time Mother was crying, and saying, 'Praise the Lord.' She told the woman of our prayers for flour, showed her the empty bin, and the crock of rising. The woman too then began to cry, and going to her buggy, she gave my brother a sack of flour, handed me a basket of potatoes, while the younger brother and sister carried in a jug of milk and a bucket of butter. 'I just thought if God was telling me to take you flour, like as not you needed the butter too, so I brought it along,' she told Mother.

"Mother kissed her, and said, 'You look like an angel to us.' Then she mixed her bread, put it to rise, and we held a real thanksgiving prayer meeting. Seeing how God had led her to help us so touched the woman that she gave her heart to Him that day in our house.

"She seemed to know Father had not been paid, so before he got home from conference, people came from all parts of his parish and paid Mother both in food and money a great deal more than they owed."

"Was that good bread?" asked Bobby as Miss Clara finished the story.

"Indeed it was," said Miss Clara, "it was like heavenly manna." ✿

G asping for air! I know the feeling.

Our family was on a picnic with some soldier friends in Panama's Canal Zone during World War II. One of the soldiers, just goofing off, threw me into the deep end of a large swimming pool—not realizing I didn't know how to swim! When I sank and didn't come up, he dived in after me. I'll never forget the desperate need for air I felt before he reached me. It took me some time to overcome my fear of water afterwards.

Inches From Air

Kent Rathbun

"The wind is blowing seventeen knots up at Lake Beardsley. Wanna go?"

"Of course."

"See you in an hour."

An hour and a half later two sailboards were perched on the roof of a Chevy station wagon. The three of us buddies laughed at each other's goofy jokes as we cruised along beneath the bright California sky.

Leaving Highway 108, we turned onto a small two-lane road that wound around in asphalt coils down to the lake. Rounding the last curve, we saw the dark-blue water of an alpine lake before us.

We were soon "toe-testing" the water, which proved to be cold—*really* cold. The early-summer sun had not yet had enough time to warm the lake to a temperature I enjoy: at least 75 degrees.

"So, uh, why don't you guys go first?" I suggested to my friends. "I'll just stay here and read a book for a while."

"Yeah, like until August, or when you think you can stand the water temperature, whichever comes first," one of the guys mocked good-naturedly.

"No, no," I said, smiling. "It's just my selfless nature to think of others first."

The guys shook their heads and headed toward the water.

They were back sooner than I'd hoped, but by that time I felt brave enough to venture forth. However, let me tell you, that first step into the water was a shocker. It felt as though all the heat I had been gathering suddenly drained out through my foot!

When I was out far enough that the back fin wouldn't drag through the mud, I climbed onto the board. The wind was strong and blew my hair into my face as I pulled up the sail and drifted away from shore. Putting down the main fin, I turned the sail to catch the wind and charged off into deeper waters.

Aside from the cold water, it was a perfect day for windsurfing: warm sunshine, windy, and beautiful. I felt great, bouncing across the whitecaps, leaving a foamy wake and fighting the pull of the wind on the sail.

Suddenly a strong gust of wind rushed toward me. The only warning I had was the sound of the spray from the whitecaps growing louder. I loosened my grip on the boom with my right hand so I could let the sail loose if necessary. This would prevent my being pulled off the board when the gust caught up with me.

Then it hit, harder than I expected. Losing my grip on the boom, I watched as it swung wide and slapped wildly in the wind. The spray from the whitecaps splashed against the back of my legs. The gust pulled me forward and off balance. I fought hard, and finally regained my grip on the boom. I leaned back, and with my right hand I pulled the boom in tight and rode the wind. I had never sailed in wind like this before: never leaned so far, ridden so fast, nor felt so powerful on the water. I was risking and conquering—so far.

The wind picked up even more. I rode it, leaning back still farther. I could feel the spray of the whitecaps wetting my hair and splashing my head. My feet were jammed into the stirrups by the pressure of my weight and the force of the wind.

Adrenaline surging, I decided to try a head dip. Pulling back still more against the boom, I tilted my head back and felt the icy water drench my scalp. Just as I tried to get up again, the wind began to die.

Struggling to regain an upright position, I soon realized I was losing the battle. I felt the freezing chill of the water engulfing me.

The sail collapsed on top of me. No problem, normally. I would simply swim out from under the sailboard. But I couldn't move my legs; my feet were stuck *above* water. With my feet high, the rest of my body sank. I was trapped underwater, inches from air.

My oxygen ran out, my lungs felt hot, and I grew panicky. Flailing and lunging at the sail, I pushed it up with my nose and grabbed a gulp of air before being pulled down again. I flailed again and drew in another deep breath. *I'm going to die!* I thought. I realized that no one could see that I was in trouble. They would simply notice a board and a sail, a common enough sight, hardly warranting a second glance.

My panic tactics wouldn't work for long—I was quickly tiring. Each attempt to struggle toward the surface for air became more difficult. I realized I would die here, today, soon!

But I hadn't panicked completely. I was stable enough to grasp the fact that giving up was a stupid choice and would not get me home for dinner with my family. So I decided to pray. I don't remember my exact words, but I'm certain that I was pretty straightforward: "God, help me or I'll die!"

Soon I felt my panic giving way to logical self-talk. *Kent, the only way out of this is to float on something or get your feet loose,* my mind seemed to say. *You don't have enough energy to keep up this panic stuff much longer. There is nothing around that you can use to float on. Since your feet are stuck on the board, you'd better unstick them.*

I relaxed under the water for a few seconds, gathering my strength before thrusting my head toward the surface one last time. I drew in as big a breath as I could and then let myself fall back without fighting. Curling up my legs made me sink lower, so I was almost upside down, looking at my calves above me. I reached up to my ankles and then to my feet. They were still stuck in the stirrups. That's what was trapping me, not the mast as I had thought.

My air was running out, and so was my energy. It was now or never. Grabbing hold of the board as best I could, I twisted it toward me. The board resisted my efforts, but I wasn't about to give up. I pulled at the board again. It moved, but not enough—my feet were still stuck and my lungs felt as if they were on fire. The panic was returning.

Reaching up again, I pulled at the board with all my strength. It tilted a little, then more . . . until finally I slipped one foot out. With one foot loose, it was easy to free the other.

My head broke through the surface of the water, and I sucked in great gulps of air. I was saved!

Clinging to the board like a shipwrecked sailor, I filled my lungs with the beautiful air that had moments before been so elusive. I thanked God for helping me to experience His peace and His presence in the midst of my panic. When my every hope was gone, He was there to rescue me. ❧

It took me many years to reach this prayer epiphany: that God does not generally respond to gimme prayers, begging prayers, imploring prayers, demanding prayers. Reason being: He will not invade our will. Only as we pray the prayer of relinquishment—not my will, but Thine be done—will He feel free to come to our rescue.

HIS WAY IN THE FIRE

Doris Thistle

Feeling that it was her duty, because of the acute need for school teachers, Miss Haven responded to a call to finish out the year in a little rural school. She had had little or no experience with rural schools and felt great need of wisdom.

Each morning when she arrived to open the little schoolhouse, as she placed the key in the door, she whispered, "Dear God, another day lies before me, and I feel so much need for your help. Please be with me and forbid that I should do anything to bring reproach to Thy name."

Then entering the room with its four rows of marked and scarred desks, she attended to her blackboard work, tidied up her desk, and with a glance at the clock, thought, *Just time enough for a little prayer before the first youngsters begin to arrive.*

Humbly she knelt before her chair, buried her face in her hands, and in the quietness of the room, with only the steady tick tock of the clock and the snapping of the fire in the background, she talked—really talked—with the Great Teacher.

But there was one late April morning that this regular program of devotions was interrupted. On her way to school the teacher overtook some of her pupils who had decided to come to school a bit earlier than usual; so she stopped her car and asked them to ride along with her. As she chatted with them and placed the key in the door, her thoughts were not upon her great need. And as she went about her routine of board work, tidying her desk, and other little tasks, the children were sandwiching in conversation about a new baby that had been born in the little village, a new dress that Hazel had been given, and other such overnight news that means so much to school children. So it was that the little talk with God was crowded out entirely.

During the opening exercises, however, as the children repeated their Bible verses and said the Lord's Prayer, Miss Haven remembered her neglect and said, "O dear God, forgive me. And do help me today." Little did she know the experience in store for her.

Since it was such a warm day in April, a number of the neighbors were mowing their lawns and burning leaves. Adjacent to the school grounds and just over the fence from the play yard there was a grove where the school children had habitually thrown paper bags, wax paper, and other trash from their lunch boxes. This had become an eyesore, and during the three weeks that the new teacher had been at the school she had been anxious to have it cleaned up. The children had assured her that it was all right to throw their trash there, but on inquiring of the chairman of the school board she had learned that he desired to have the practice stopped and the ground cleared.

The morning studies were over and the regular time for the Friday afternoon civic club meeting arrived. Miss Haven spoke to the children about the matter of cleaning up the grove. Gladly they responded, and bands were formed and set to work, so that in seemingly no time the waste material had been brought into the center of the schoolyard and piled for burning. Orders were given for two pails of water to be brought, brooms and sticks were sought out, and with six of the older boys on guard, the fire was set. Within a very short time the waste had become ashes, and water was poured over the remains. It was too early to dismiss school, so the children were summoned into the schoolroom to finish the afternoon with a program of songs and speaking. Two of the older boys volunteered to clean up the ashes that remained in the center of the yard and carry them away. In short order, they were back to join in the fun.

About a half hour later an agitated neighbor burst into the room and announced. "Do you know that the woods down the road are all afire, and there's not a soul to help fight the blaze?" Instantly, the teacher gave orders for the little folks to be taken care of while she, with a group of older boys and girls, armed themselves with brooms and sticks and hastened to the scene.

The dump where the boys had disposed of the ashes was at the edge of the woods. Undoubtedly, the ashes that had been disposed there had caused the outburst of flames that now was traveling in all directions and endangering the farmhouse across the field.

"Boys and girls, do your best—beat the flames with your brooms, and be careful not to get burned," the anxious teacher shouted. Then she rushed away to see what other help could be found. However, there was a war at the time, and all the men were eight miles away, working in the shipyard. Realizing how helpless the situation was, she recalled that "man's extremity is God's opportunity." She rushed into the little schoolhouse, threw herself down before her swivel chair, and cried out in anguish. "O dear God, please send help. Please don't let the fire get up to that farmhouse. I've made a terrible mistake—been so unwise. Please forgive me, and please, oh, please, God, check this fire."

Then she arose, looked out the window, and as though to defeat her courage, the flames seemed to be reaching higher and angrier than ever.

Again she sank to her knees and cried, "Dear Father, you are able to do what I have asked. Please grant my request in such a way that those boys and girls down there who are beating the flames will know it was You who put it out. Please, please—"

This time as she looked out the window, she saw a man hastening down the road with a large hand pump and extinguisher. As she watched, she prayed. The efforts of one man and the small band of children seemed so puny. The field was as dry as tinder and was burning rapidly!

Dear me, thought the teacher, *can it be that God did not hear me—is not going to answer?*

A third time she bowed in prayer, *this* time saying, "Dear Father, I leave it with you. I know nothing is too hard for you. And now, dear Father, if it be Thy will, let these children know that Thou art able to do great things."

Was that the door she heard opening? Yes, and in came her little band of boys and girls, smeared with smoke, flourishing their brooms (some of them by now mere broomsticks). They crowded around their teacher and shouted, "All out!"

"But," added Charlie, "we never could have done it if we hadn't known you were here praying. One of the boys peeked in the window to see why you weren't down fighting the fire with us, and he came running back and told us you were fighting it on your knees. He told us, 'Teacher's up there praying; so keep fighting.' "

Tears welled up in Miss Haven's eyes as she bowed her hand and said with a choking voice, "Thank you, dear God, for helping them."

And little Dean, who never could seem to master his English, added, "God done it all right, but we helped Him!" ❧

*M*y minister / missionary father, Lawrence Wheeler, was a prayer warrior like Aunt Liza. Whenever he reached the end of his rope, he always turned to God, perfectly confident that He would address the matter in His own way. He knew God would never let him down.

A 1940 Miracle

Phyllis Prout

Mrs. Fuller was standing by the telephone in her sunny kitchen, listening intently to the news that was being conveyed over the wire. Her kind, weather-beaten face registered deep concern.

"I'm glad you told me about that poor family, Mrs. Higgins," she commented after her friend had paused for breath. "I'll run right over to Aunt Liza's, and she'll help me get some clothes and food together for them. You know, every year she cans hundreds of quarts of fruit and vegetables, just so she can have plenty to give away whenever she hears of someone in need. Tell them not to worry; we'll bring food and clothing."

Hastily she removed an old sweater from a hook on the wall, slipped it on, tied a scarf over her head, and walked quickly in the direction of her nearest neighbor, Aunt Liza, who lived alone on a five-acre farm. As she neared the modest white cottage, surrounded by colorful flowers, she quickened her steps. She knocked vigorously on the back door, for Aunt Liza was

very deaf. After repeated knockings, the door was opened, and there was Aunt Liza's cheerful face wreathed in smiles, her brown eyes snapping and twinkling.

"Why, Mary Fuller, I'm glad to see you," she shouted with enthusiasm. "How could you leave your chores so early in the morning?"

By this time, Mrs. Fuller was able to catch her breath.

"I felt I just *must* run over and tell you about the poor family around the next bend—you know, the ones who live in the auto camp. The father is out of work, and the mother is sick, and they need food and clothing. I knew you would want to know about it."

"Land sakes," exclaimed Aunt Liza, starting for the cellar where she kept her canned food, "come down and help me put up a box for them right now. You know, I can everything that I don't sell from this place, and then my son-in-law, who is manager of a market in the city, brings me all the leftover fruits and vegetables that can't be sold, and I put them up too, so I can give them to the poor. I always say it is a sin to let anything go to waste."

"I don't see how you do so much, Aunt Liza, when you attend to practically all your own farm work."

"I always say the Lord fits the back to the burden, my dear," replied Aunt Liza, "and I praise Him every day for giving me strength. I'll go over to the camp with you and see if I can give the poor woman some treatments. You know, I often get people interested in the Lord."

This instance is typical of Aunt Liza—always energetic, cheerful, praising God, and thinking of others more than of herself. The fact that she shouts because of her deafness only serves to give her a hearty, enthusiastic manner. She is truly one of God's saints, a real missionary in her community. She regards God as a friend, and takes all her troubles to Him. He rewards her trusting faith and hears her prayers.

One morning Aunt Liza rose early to irrigate her berries, which were soon to be ready for market and which would account for a large part of her income for the year. The water was supplied for her farm by a very fine artesian well. Each farm in this community had its own well, and the farmers were justly proud of the water.

This morning Aunt Liza was happily humming a hymn as she turned the switch of the pump and then went to put on her heavy boots before going into the berry patch. Imagine her surprise and dismay when she returned and found that although the pump was working, no water was coming out of the well. She hastened over to the Fullers' farm to see if Mr. Fuller could help her, for Aunt Liza had no money to pay a repairman. When she arrived at her neighbors' farm, she found great excitement there.

"Aunt Liza, do you have water?" inquired Mr. Fuller. "Our well seems to have gone dry."

"Why, that's just exactly why I came over to see you," exclaimed Aunt Liza. "Something has gone wrong with my well, too."

Inquiry around the neighborhood revealed the fact that *all* the wells had gone dry, so an expert was called in to investigate the cause. They anxiously awaited his report.

When he inspected Aunt Liza's well, he said, "Yes, yours is just like the others. The water level in this neighborhood has dropped down much lower than it was formerly, and the only way to get water is to dig your wells deeper. Do you wish me to have someone come out to dig yours?"

Aunt Liza's heart sank. There was no money for this emergency, and her berries needed irrigating *immediately!* A few days' delay might seriously injure the crop.

"No," she replied, "I have no money for that."

"But what are you going to do for water?" he asked.

"I don't know," replied Aunt Liza, "except to do what I always do in cases of emergency. I shall pray to my God about it. I know that He can help me out of this trouble, even as He has helped me in times of trouble in the past."

The engineer laughed. "I'm afraid you'll need to do more than pray in this case," he said skeptically, "for the water just isn't there anymore. I'm afraid that you don't understand the gravity of the situation." He then disconnected the pump at the well, and as he turned to leave, he said, "Well, call me up when you decide what you're going to do."

Aunt Liza took her trouble to her Friend, who had never failed her in any crisis. She talked to Him as she would to an earthly friend, whom she could see face to face, and laid the whole burden upon Him. That night in a dream she saw an angel standing by her bed. The angel said, "There is water in your well now."

She awakened immediately after this dream and began to praise and thank God, for Aunt Liza's faith knew no doubt, and she was confident that the water was now in her well.

The next morning she called the engineer out to see her. He came, thinking that she was at last ready to make arrangements to have her well dug deeper. However, her first words disillusioned him. She said, "Mr. Nelson, I want you to start my pump."

Mr. Nelson was alarmed, as he feared that too much worry might have affected his elderly client's reason. Gently he began to explain the situation again. He said, "There is no use in turning the pump on, madam, as there is no water there."

However, no words of his could change Aunt Liza's mind, and when she persisted in her demand, he decided to humor her, thinking that this was the best way to prove that she was wrong. He went out to the well, connected the pump again, and turned it on. Out gushed an abundant stream of water, clear and sparkling.

"Thank the Lord!" exclaimed Aunt Liza. "I knew He had answered my prayer!"

The well expert could not speak. Never had he witnessed such a phenomenon. After Aunt Liza had told him of her dream, he replied, "God *must* have answered your prayer, for this is a miracle. No other well in the neighborhood has water."

Aunt Liza's gratitude to her heavenly Father knew no bounds, and she told the story of God's kindness to all the community. The engineer carried the news to the city hall, and some of the officials came out to investigate. Aunt Liza told each one about her God and how He hears and answers prayer.

Many times when we read of answered prayer, we think that such experiences came to people many years ago or in a mission field far away, but this modern miracle happened in the year 1940, in the western part of the United States. ❧

*T*his was the last story added to this collection. I was convicted that I should share it with you.

This story took place during the summer of 2002 in the Colorado Rockies. Since snowfall amounts had climbed to normal by May, we felt hopeful that we might make it through summer and fall without any major forest fires. The problem is that it takes only three days of sustained high winds to turn the state tinder-dry no matter how much snow accumulated early on.

Alas! the safe summer was not to be. On June 9 someone near Lake George failed to extinguish a campfire completely. Within only hours it had exploded across three thousand acres—and it showed no signs of stopping. All Coloradans trembled as television stations went into 24/7 coverage.

The very next day, we had some unexpected guests: Because of the commanding view to be had from our front deck (of a 150-mile stretch of the Front Range), we were visited by Channel 31 FOX television reporters and camera-people, FEMA, and Elk Creek Fire Department personnel. We were interviewed by FOX reporters as well. Needless to say, the subject on everyone's mind was What if? What if the fire should sweep north across Highway 285 into the Bailey, Conifer, Morrison, Evergreen corridor, putting some sixty thousand people at risk? What should area homeowners do, in terms of defensible space, to improve their odds of surviving such a fast-moving fire? And *we* were the poster child: they told us what trees we needed to deal with *soon*.

By June 10 (the following day), no small thanks to high winds, the fire (now redubbed "The Hayman Fire") had scorched seventy-five thousand acres and all the dwellings within its path. Inexorably, it would keep on growing over the next month, until it became the largest forest fire in Colorado history.

Meanwhile, for those farther away from the fire, life went on. But always *everyone* remained conscious of the possibility of sudden wind-shifts. At one time, we decided to escape the smoke-filled sky and spend a few days in Estes Park (about eighty miles north of us) and Rocky Mountain National Park. We felt comfortable in doing so because the fire was still some distance away from Conifer. But one morning while we were in Estes Park, the wind began picking up velocity. On everyone's mind was which way the fire would go. Then came a news bulletin that pre-empted everything else on television: "Attention Everyone! Winds are reaching seventy miles an hour, and we won't see any lessening of their speed until—[x number of hours away]. The fire is now racing directly for the Highway 285 corridor. All those individuals in that vicinity ought to be ready to evacuate on fifteen minutes' notice."

We could only look at each other in shock, for our home was more than two hours away! And even had we been able to reach it in time, we knew we wouldn't be able to get through the roadblocks. We later discovered that to be true: only emergency vehicles were permitted in.

So all we could do was pray. We asked the Lord that, if it be His will, He would stop or redirect the wind in time. We reminded Him that our library archives were now at risk; if they were to burn up, that would mean the probable end of our story ministry. Well, not *our* story ministry—His. Always it has been *His*.

So what about all our other possessions? If we had only fifteen minutes to prepare, what would we take with us? What would we leave behind? Long before, we'd discussed such an eventuality. As for what we or our children loved most, it would be Connie's hand-stitched quilts, some old photograph albums, perhaps the sea-scape painting we all loved, and a basket of ancient blocks eight generations of Wheeler children had played with. Other than that, it would be only life, sweet life, that mattered. It is indeed a sobering experience to be forced to prioritize in only a few minutes all that you value most in life.

Later on, neighbors filled us in on what happened next. Everyone on Conifer Mountain was waiting for that dreaded phone call giving them fifteen minutes to pack up and leave. Many—even nominal Christians—were on their knees. The fire chiefs would write off the entire mountain had the wind-driven fire jumped Highway 285—reason being that the mountain was so steep that once the fire reached the north side, nothing on earth could have stopped it.

Then, four full hours before the wind was predicted to diminish, and just as suddenly as if someone had flicked a giant switch in the sky, and just as the fire was racing towards Highway 285, the wind stopped. Shortly afterwards, a freak light snow began falling.

Sometime later I was told, "Joe, did you realize that down south in Colorado Springs, the entire Focus on the Family ministry was on their knees asking the Lord to stop the fire before it burned up your irreplaceable story archives?"

God watches over His own! ❧

SECTION THREE

"Don't worry about anything; instead,
pray about everything. Tell God what you need,
and thank him for all he has done."
—Philippians 4:6, NLT

"God has infinite tolerance for our requests and
demands, especially those supporting the cause of
God's own kingdom. Why else would the Bible
include so many importuning psalms,
so many prophetic laments?"
—Yancey, page 149

There are moments in life that seem to last days, and days that last years. George Bond shares such a disaster in this riveting account. For him it proved to be a life-changing epiphany; vicariously, that may be true for the reader as well.

THE CASTAWAY OF FISH ROCK

George Bond

Hairbreadth escapes, did you say, sir? Ah, yes, I s'pose we've all had more or less of 'em, but maybe sailors knows more about 'em than people livin' on the land ever can. Don't you think so, sir?"

We were on our way home together from a week-night prayer meeting, Solomon French and I, under the bright, crisp starlight of the Newfoundland winter night, the frosty ground ringing under our feet and the clear air blowing sharply upon our faces as we walked briskly along. Solomon was a fisherman, and a splendid specimen of his class, too; broad shoulders and well-knit frame giving evidence of great strength and power of endurance, while his fine open features, with a smile of good-natured happiness beaming out from them, and his clear blue eyes, full of frankness and intelligence, won your sympathetic liking and confidence on the shortest acquaintance. A good man was Solomon, a genuinely earnest and whole-souled Christian; warm-hearted and thoroughgoing in his practical devotion to God and duty.

Deep spiritual experiences had come into his life and hallowed and mellowed his character as only such experiences can, giving it an elevation and breadth that raised him above and beyond the commonplace and monotonous level of ordinary Christian life. In our short acquaintance, I had already been struck with the rare insight and outlook of his views, the richness and wisdom of his understanding of divine things, the simplicity and comprehensiveness of his faith, and the clear common sense of his practical piety; and I saw in these the secret of the great respect in which he was held, and the strong influence for good that he exerted in the community.

On the night in question, the service had turned—the hymns particularly—upon divine providence and the presence of God with His people in times of danger and distress, and our conversation, as we trudged homeward from the meeting, had naturally followed the line of our previous thoughts.

"Why, sir," continued Solomon, "as we were singin' that verse tonight,

> 'Oft hath the sea confessed Thy power,
> And given me back at Thy command;
> It could not, Lord, my life devour,
> Safe in the hollow of Thy hand,'

my mind was busy enough with more than one experience of my own in my nearly forty years of knockin' about on the sea. Many a time I've seen God's hand plain enough. 'Deed I have. But when you started that verse, at the close of the meetin', sir, 'Though waves and storms go o'er my head,' I fairly broke down and cried, for it seemed to me God was remindin' me once more of His great love and care for me in a time when I sung that verse in a different place from where we was tonight. Indeed, I can never sing that hymn or hear it sung without thinkin' of it. Someday I'll tell you about it, sir."

"Come in, now," said I, for by this time we had reached my own door and my friend was preparing to bid me good night. "Come in now, Solomon; I've heard something about that wonderful escape of yours, and I would like to hear of it from your own lips."

"Well, sir," said Solomon, when, a few minutes later, we were seated cozily before my sitting room fire, "so you've heard some-thing of the story of the Fish Rock? 'Tis a strange story and a solemn one, too; an' I can never tell it, even at this distance o' time, without feelin' a good deal. In the spring of 1872, I shipped for the sealing voyage—for the ice, as we say—in the brig *Huntsman* of Bay Roberts, in Conception Bay. Captain Dawe was the master, and there was a crew of sixty of us, all told. A good ship we had under us, an' an experienced man for our captain—a real old seal killer. We left port about the fifth of March, and near the vicinity of the Grey Islands we got about half a load of seals, but the seals were not plenty, an' we were long time doin' little, so the captain concluded to go on further north as the season was gettin' late, an' try for some old seals, so we ran down to the Labrador coast.

"Just as we got down, a gale o' wind sprung up, with a ter'ble heavy sea, and it got so rough that we couldn't stand in the open water, an' was forced to put into the ice for shelter—that is, sir, into a string of loose running ice about three or four miles off the shore.

"There was a couple of other crafts not far from us, an' they put into the ice as well. 'Twas bad enough for us, you may believe, sir, but 'twas the only thing we could do in the ter'ble heavy wind an' sea, to get into the ice, where, of course, it was smoother. We was far enough off the land, bein' on the outer edge of the ice to keep us from fearin' the lee shore, an' barrin' the danger of runnin' into an iceberg, we was fairly safe, we thought, for we had no idea of rocks at that distance from the shore. But once in the ice, of course, we had to go with it, helpless as you may say, for there was a strong tide runnin' along the shore as well as the heavy wind an' sea. Ugly enough it looked, sir, I tell 'ee, as might come on, an' no sign of improvement—getting worse it was, indeed all the time.

"We had some narrow escapes from icebergs as we drove along with the wind an' tide; but, as I said just now, we never thought of rocks.

" 'Twas several hours after dark, and we was drivin' along, every man of us anxiously lookin' out into the darkness when we saw what we took to be an iceberg some distance ahead. All of a sudden one of the crew sings out, 'Rock! Rock on the lee bow!'

" 'Twas no iceberg, sir, but the sea an' ice breakin' over a reef of rock right ahead of us. Quick as thought, the captain sang out to back the headsails but 'twas no use, we drove on right fair for the rock.

" 'God have mercy on us,' says the captain, 'we're lost. Let every man try to save himself!'

"It was an awful time, sir; sixty men of us there on the deck of that ship drivin' right into the jaws of death, for there was no chance of escape that we could see. Some four or five men jumped from the weather bow, but were smashed up at once. More took the riggin'. With some others, I ran out on the main boom, but couldn't see a pan of ice big enough to jump on, so I said to myself, 'I'm as well here as anywhere else.' Talk about religion, sir, I felt thankful then for my interest in Christ, an' I was as happy as I am in this room this minute.

"I was standin' there holdin' on by the topping lift when she struck bow on against the rock; an' as she reeled back from the blow, her stern went under the sea an' ice, and I found myself rollin' over an' over among the breakers that were dashing up over the rock. I couldn't have thought it possible, sir, for a man to live a minute among the pounding, grinding ice an' sea, but I did. As it dashed me up on the rock, I got hold of the kelp an' stuff that was about it, an' held on for dear life. But the sea came in and dashed me away. Again I got hold, an' again the sea carried me away. I got another grip, however, an' held on, desperate, for I felt my strength givin' way, an' I knew I couldn't hold out agen' many more seas. But again the sea dashed over me, an' swept me off, and I gave myself up for lost. But I managed to get hold again, a bit higher up, an' I said to myself—I felt that much exhausted—'If another sea takes me off, I'm gone; I haven't any more strength left.'

"Well, sir, the next sea came in to my feet, an' no further, an' sea after sea broke on the rock an' rolled that far, but not far enough to sweep me off. It was a kind of point of the rock, just big enough for me to rest my hip on the top of it, and half sit, half lie, just out of reach of the sea.

"I say out of reach of the sea, an' so I was, so far of carryin' me away went, though I didn't know when a bigger sea than usual might sweep me off, and the blinding spray was dashin' over me constantly. There I was alone on that wild rock, drenched with icy water, bruised and bleedin' from the awful beatin' I had had when cast ashore, holdin' on for dear life in the darkness and storm. Half an hour before on the deck of our vessel, in the midst of my friends; an' now, so far as I knew, the only one living out of them all.

"It was pitch dark; I could see nothin' but the white breakers as they dashed up to my feet, an' I could hear nothin' but the howlin' of the wind, the roarin' of the sea, an' the awful groanin' an' shriekin' of the ice. An' yet, sir, I thank God, I was kept in peace. He was near me. I felt His hand sustainin' and helpin' me, an' I sung about them words we sung tonight:

" 'Though waves and storms go o'er my head,

Though strength and health and friends be gone,
Though joys be withered all, and dead,
Though every comfort be withdrawn,
On this my steadfast soul relies,
Father, Thy mercy never dies.'

"You don't wonder, sir, that I can't sing those words or hear 'em sung without re-memberin' that ter'ble time. Yet, blessed be God, He kept me, as I said, in peace. O how glad I was that I knew Him, that I loved Him, that I had been tryin' to serve Him. How glad I was that through it all I could feel around an' underneath me the everlastin' arms.

"It was dark, indeed, around me, sir, but I had wonderful views on that rock. I could see life as I never saw it before, the value of it, the need of a man livin' wholly for God an' in read-iness for whatever might happen, an' the awful foolishness of livin' for anything else, busy about this thing an' that thing, an' leaving the most important of all things neglected. I had been servin' God, sir, but there, in the dark-ness, there come to me such wonderful thoughts about God, an' the importance of livin' for Him, that I felt as I never felt before how poor my service had been, an' how different my life might be made if I had it to live over again. An' yet, blessed be His name, I had the assurance of His love, an' favor, an' forgiveness. Jesus was with me, an' I rested on His arm.

"Well, the long night wore away, and when mornin' broke I could see somethin' of where I was. It was a dreary sight, sure enough. The ice was hove up all around me, but the wind an' sea was droppin' somewhat. The rock I was on was about fifteen feet high, an' less than a quarter of a mile long—just a low, narrow reef of rock almost covered by the sea an' ice. I could make out the hills on the mainland four or five miles or more across the ice, a rocky, desolate-lookin' coast, but not a sign of a ship or of a human bein', livin' or dead, in all the miles of ice around me. I was alone, famished, bruised, half dead, on that bit of a rock in the midst of the icy sea. I was so sore that I felt as if I couldn't stir, an' so weak that I felt as if I had no strength to do so if I wished. The sea was smoother, an' the day got clear, but there seemed little chance of anything happenin' to help me. I was beyond human help, to all appearance. Many a time that day I sat up well as I could and looked all around to see if I could see any sign of help or hope, but there was nothin' to be seen but the miles of ice and the distant shore.

"It was a long day, sir, a long day. Stiff an' sore as I was, it was nothing to the pangs of hunger that began to seize me as the day wore on. That was the worst of all. It was indescribable; I couldn't tell you what I suffered. So I made up my mind that, as the sea continued goin' down, I'd try to crawl ashore next mornin'. It was a poor chance of my gettin' there, an' a poor chance of my gettin' to any settlement if I did; but I felt I couldn't hold out much longer on the rock, an' that very soon I wouldn't have any strength to leave it. I'd perish if I stopped, an' I could only perish if I fell through the ice or failed to get to any place where people was livin'; so I said to myself, I'll try anyway in the mornin', please God.

"I didn't give up heart, you see, sir, at all, though everything looked so black. Seemin' to me God kept me from despair an' sinkin' down under my desperate condition. I prayed to Him hearty an' often, an' sung a hymn now an' then to brighten myself up. Well, the second night passed much like the first, except that the sea had gone down and the spray didn't dash over me at all, and I could lie a bit more comfortable on the rock. But I was ter'ble sore an' cold, an' hunger was gnawin' at me more an' more. When mornin' came, the second dawnin' I'd seen on that rock, I saw that it was goin' to be a fine day, an' that the sea was smoother than ever. I looked out an' saw a good big pan of ice a little distance off from where I was lyin', so, with a prayer for God's help an' guidance, I crawled off to it and started for the shore.

"It was slow work, sir, you may depend. I was that sore an' weak, it was ter'ble labor. I'd get over two or three pans an' then take a spell; then, maybe, go twice the breadth of this room, an' then stop for another spell. I suppose, in three hours or more, I wasn't a mile away from the rock. You see, I was beat about wonderful, an' felt my legs givin' out with weakness. However, I hobbled along, takin' short walks and then restin', but makin' poor headway. I didn't give up, though, not a bit, an' I was sittin' down takin' off my outer clothing to relieve myself of its weight, for it was all water-soaked an' iced up, when just as I was goin' to start again, I heard voices, and lookin' up, I saw three or four men comin' across the ice towards me. 'Twas a glad sight you may depend, sir, an' a very unexpected one, an' my heart gave big beats of thankfulness an' excitement. I felt that my troubles was over. They had come from the shore on purpose to reach an' save me, and they was ter'ble glad when they saw me.

"How do you suppose they came to know I was on the rock? Well, sir, 'twas wonderful. They told me the rock I was on was what is called the Fish Rock, off Cape Charles, which was the high land I had seen while lyin' there, an' Captain Graham in the sealin' steamer had been in Cape Charles harbor during the gale, and after it was over had happened to be up on the cape with his spyglass lookin' out over the ice. He, or some of his men, caught sight of something movin' on the rock, an' at first thought it was only a seal, but after a while believed it was a man. So they determined to get him, if possible. They set fire to a tar barrel so that the man on the rock might see it an' know where was people not far off, an' then the captain got about forty men to start out over the ice next mornin' and try to get to him and bring him ashore. So they found me, sir, as I've told you.

"Well, they gave me a little bread and changed my old water-soaked boots, an' I felt stronger, so with their help an' in one spell more I got to the land. But I couldn't stand when I got there, an' they had to hand me up. Captain Graham was wonderful kind to me, took me into his cabin and cared for me like as if I was his brother. But I was very ill an' a mass of bruises an' cuts, body and head. I was a poor sight to look at, an' I remember the captain would not let me see the lookin'glass because he was afraid I'd be frightened at my own looks.

"They brought me home in the steamer on her return, an' by the time I got there I was beginnin' to mend fast. But it was a long time before I was much good. I went about on two crutches all spring and part of the summer, but by the end of it I was able to walk without 'em; an' now, sir, I never feel any ill effects of my dreadful exposure, except sometimes in my feet. I was on that rock, sir, from about nine o'clock Sunday night till about eleven on Tuesday morning.

"It wasn't till I got back home that I knew whether any others than myself had been saved from the *Huntsman,* but I found that eighteen of 'em had got home before me; so there were just nineteen of us saved out of the crew of sixty. When the vessel struck an' her stern went under the water, most of the crew was drowned or beat to pieces with the ice as the sea dashed over her, but some managed to get on the ice an' crawl off on the weather side. Many of these got smashed up between the ice, but eighteen of 'em reached a craft that was drivin' along a little distance from us, and bein' further out, fortunately, was able to clear the rock. This craft, the *Rescue,* which, strangely enough, happened to be commanded by our captain's brother, got safely home a couple of weeks before I did, but our own captain an' his son, with all the rest of our crew, perished in the breakers at the Fish Rock, or were smashed to pieces in the drifting ice after the vessel went down.

"Sir, you have my story. I can never forget that experience, never, never! If any man should be thankful to God, it is me. If any man should love and serve Him faithfully, surely I ought. God was with me on the Fish Rock, an' He is with me today. Many a time in the storm an' calm of the years that have passed since then I've proved Him to be a God near at hand and not afar off; an' bless His name, I find Him so still. An' when I tell my story, sir, an' I've told it many a time in these years since it happened, mostly to seafaring men like myself, I do so want to tell it that those who hear it may see the value of faith in Christ, an' the power of God to keep a man's soul in peace in the midst of the greatest danger an' distress. I do want to help them to seek that power, if they don't already possess it, an' to have their faith in it strengthened, if they already do. There's nothin' but the religion of the Lord Jesus Christ can keep a man straight, an' safe, an' happy, blow high or blow low, in rough water or smooth, below or aloft, afloat or ashore."

What if two individuals pray for the same thing and both sincerely believe God will answer in their favor? This old story does just that. I have discovered that very few prayer stories address such an issue. It is reminiscent of an issue Abraham Lincoln wrote about long ago.

Both the North and the South prayerfully urged God to help their side win the Civil War. How was God to choose? Lincoln wrote, "Both read the same Bible, and pray to the same God; and each invokes His aid against the other. . . . The prayers of both could not be answered; that of neither has been answered fully. The Almighty has His own purposes."

THE OTHER BOY

Jeanette Swing

Mamma, Mamma," exclaimed Tom at the top of his voice. As Tom had a voice with a great deal of "top" to it, the baby gave a jump and began to cry. Tom's mamma, half smiling, half frowning at his excitement, set him to rocking the cradle. He had to wait until the little one was asleep before he could tell the news that was so hard to keep.

"Well, Tom," said his mother finally.

"Why, Mamma, I'm almost sure of that place in Mr. Lawrence's store, almost sure. And won't it be fine! He pays five dollars a week.* That will be a great help to us, won't it!"

"Yes, indeed," said his mother. "It will be a great help. Besides, I've always wanted you to get in a good place like that, where you can work your way up and show them what a faithful boy you are, even if you do wake the baby sometimes."

"Oh, I was excited, Mamma," said the boy, smiling. "You can understand how a fellow feels when he has been trying so long to get a position, and then has this nice one almost as good as promised to him."

"It is not quite certain, though, Tom?" asked his mother.

"No, not quite, though I feel pretty sure of it, now; Mr. Lawrence said that he had to see another boy yet who was anxious for the place, but he felt that I would suit him and for me to come in the morning."

Tom and his mother were in pretty good spirits all that evening, and many were the things thought of and planned in regard to the new position; and Tom told how faithful he meant to be, and how Mr. Lawrence should never regret having given him the position.

At last bedtime came, and though Tom was certain he could not sleep a wink for thinking about it, yet his mother advised him

---

* About the equivalent of one hundred dollars a week in today's money.

to go to bed and try, so that he would be energetic and alert the next day.

"Mother," he said, as he was leaving the room, "I want to ask you something. God always answers our prayers, doesn't He?"

"Yes, dear, if it is best to have them answered."

"Well, it certainly will be best for *me* to have this job, and I've been praying for it ever since I first heard of it, and I'm certain God will answer this prayer. Don't you think He will?"

"I hope so, Tom. It seems for the best, and I think He will."

The next morning Tom was up bright and early and could hardly wait to eat his breakfast so eager was he to get to the store and be made perfectly certain of the position that meant so much to him and his widowed mother. He had prayed for it more earnestly than ever before, and so had the boy's mother, and both were sure that their prayers would be answered.

Tom kissed the baby and hurried away, thinking of the pretty little new shoes he meant to buy for her out of that wonderful five dollars he was to earn the first week, and how the baby would laugh and crow as no other baby ever could, according to Tom's opinion. He was an unselfish little fellow, and thought more of the good things he would get for the baby and Mother than any good it

would bring to himself.

In about an hour after he had gone, his mother was in the kitchen washing dishes, when she heard the side door open and close, but no Tom came rushing in to tell her the good news. All was very quiet in the little sitting room.

Tom's mother wiped her hands, picked up the baby, and went in, and there in the chair before the fire sat Tom, with his face bowed in his hands and the hot tears trickling through his fingers.

He looked up at his mother and tried to smile at the baby that crowed at him and didn't seem to know what to make of his serious face.

"Well, Mamma," he said rather huskily, "the other boy got the job."

"I'm sorry," she said, unable to keep the tears from her own eyes.

"And I'm never going to pray for anything again," said Tom, his face taking on a hard look.

"Tom," said his mother, "you don't mean that, I'm sure."

"No, Mamma, I can hardly mean that, but it doesn't seem to be any use to pray for things if we don't get them. I'm certain it would have been best for me to have had it, and I just don't understand."

Tom's mother was a simple woman and didn't know how to explain it herself. In fact, she felt very much disappointed that Tom hadn't gotten the job, and she couldn't quite feel that everything had happened for the best.

Several weeks passed before Tom secured a position in another store—one that wasn't half so nice as the one he wanted and was certain he should have had.

One day his proprietor sent him on an errand to a very poor part of the city to collect a bill from a woman there. "It's not likely she'll pay you," he said, "for they're as poor as can be, or else they don't want to pay, but I'm not going to give them any peace until they do. I have been sending collectors there right along for the last three months."

Tom found the place—a dirty, crowded tenement house. The woman lived in the very top of it. The stairs were dark and steep, and Tom was quite out of breath when he reached the room he had been directed to.

The woman who admitted him had a baby in her arms and another little one clinging to her skirts, and there were three more children playing about on the floor. The room wasn't dirty, but it was very poor and ugly, and Tom couldn't help thinking how awful it must be to live in such a little place, and how different their own little sitting room at home was, al-

though it wasn't very elegant either.

"Come in," said the woman when Tom told her he was collecting for the coal sold by the Crown Company. He went in and was glad to sit down.

The woman gave the baby to its sister to hold, and then she said at last, "I'm so glad that I can pay Mr. Brown. You can tell him, please, that my son has got work now, and that I'm sorry he had to wait for the money. It is a terrible thing to be out of work, and Ben tried so hard to get something to do."

"Is that your son you spoke of?" asked Tom, feeling interested in the woman and thinking what a pretty baby it was and how it made him think of the one at home.

"Yes, Ben is my son, and one of the best boys a woman ever had. But the factory where he worked burned down, and we came near starving and freezing last winter. And Ben was beginning to think that he never would get another place. Times have been so hard and so many people out of work, but it came at last. I often tell Ben it was because we prayed so hard, and I always knew that God would answer our prayers, and so He did at last."

Tom was silent for a moment, thinking. Eventually, he asked, "Where does your son work?"

"For Mr. Lawrence, the grocer," the woman answered. "I don't know what we would have done if he'd not gotten the place, for we were facing starvation."

When Tom went home that night, he said to his mother:

"Well, Mamma, a strange thing happened today. You know ever since I didn't get that position at Mr. Lawrence's, I've been harboring hard feelings toward that boy who did get it, and I've been thinking it was no use praying for things because you know how we prayed for that and it was given to someone else. Well, today I came across the home of the other fellow, and I declare, he needed it lots worse than I did. Why, there is his mother and four or five little children, all living in one room, and such an awful place it is! And they were pretty nearly starving. And the strange thing is that this fellow and his mother were both praying for the position, just the same as we were. Of course, God couldn't give it to us both, and He knew which of us needed it most." ❧

*D*r. Eric B. Hare has to have been the most mesmerizing storyteller I heard during all my growing-up years. Not just in voice tonality and expression, but also in vibrant eyes, flailing arms, perambulating feet, and eyebrows that twitched more expressively than did those of any other human I have ever known. He and his wife were missionaries to what was then known as Burma (now Myanmar).

We are all perpetually losing things—but this particular loss would be devastating!

THE JUNGLE BANDMASTER

Eric B. Hare

"One, two, three, four, five, six, seven, eight."

"Hold on, porter, there's one more piece—a basket!"

"No, sir! Your ticket says eight pieces. That's all you put in."

"But the basket! It's got my cornet in it, porter—"

"Well, I'm very sorry for you, mister, but it isn't usual to expect more out of a cloakroom than you put in. You'd better inform the police."

"Inform the what?"

"Inform the police."

"Then is it really truly lost?"

The realization of the awful truth, the mental checking up only to find the porter's statements correct, made me dizzy. No, stopping to think, I couldn't remember seeing the basket when we got off the train in the morning. I may as well confess to start with that I'm the jungle bandmaster, and though it doesn't sound nice to tell a story about one-self, yet it can't be helped this time. I'm the one who lost his cornet, and, oh, how sick I felt over it all!

Here we were on our way to the Taikgyi (Burma) meeting. The good pastor over there wanted some help with the music. But now it was gone. Gone! The cornet that had inspired the jungle band and that had played in a hundred villages—*gone!* I've seen some disheartened people in my life, but if ever you come across a sicker-looking individual than a jungle bandmaster who has lost his cornet, then I don't want to meet him.

I informed the police. I informed the station master, and I searched the station and the lost luggage room. I asked every coolie within hearing distance if he had seen my basket. Of course, there was only one basket. There could be only one basket, ever, and that was the basket that had my cornet in it. But not a soul had seen such a basket all day long. Neither had I. That was just the whole trouble. The basket was lost, I tell you, and my cornet was *gone!*

Lifelessly, I put my eight pieces of luggage into the gharri and directed the gharri wallah* to the mission house. Even had the hour of death been nigh, I couldn't have felt more hopelessly dejected than I did then—till my soul reacted with the thought of prayer. Why, of course! Man's extremity—God's opportunity. That sounded brighter. Why not pray! So right there, in that old gharri, rumbling off down the road, mingling with the thousand sounds and voices common to an Eastern street, I prayed—a real prayer.

I told the Lord that that cornet was just as much His as it was mine. I told Him that it was just as good a preacher as I was. And then, as we talked the situation over together, I dared to ask Him that if it could glorify His name, if it could benefit His cause, to please have it sent back that evening, as I wanted to take it to the Taikgyi meeting the next day.

Now that was just 3:30 P.M.

Talking it all over with the Lord lifted my burden and gave me the assurance that God was now going to take matters into His hands. Maybe He would teach me a severe lesson, but I felt safe in the hands of the Lord because He always works things out for our good in the long run. I was in this frame of mind when I completed the journey to the mission house, where my wife, sharing my disappointments and hopes, helped me get things ready for the night.

Now listen.

At 5 P.M., while we were thus engaged, there was a knock on the door, and a Mr. Minus, a total stranger to me, stood there asking for Mr. Hare. Yes, he had the basket. A friend of his, traveling in the ladies' compartment with my wife, had by mistake taken it with her luggage. She had remembered my wife's name from the reservation ticket on the carriage, and in conversation had learned that we were Adventists. This had enabled Mr. Minus to trace us from the church to the pastor's residence, then to the office, and finally to the mission house where we were staying. He declared that his friend had given him no peace till he had started off in a gharri to hunt us up.

But just a minute, young people, I want to ask you a question. Just why did our friend wait till 3:30 before starting out to hunt us? Just what was it that made him start exactly at 3:30 P.M.?

If you could have heard the jungle bandmaster blowing that old cornet of his at the Taikgyi meeting, you would have thought that it sounded as if he knew something about the whys and wherefores of it, all right. ❧

---

* Driver of a horse-drawn cab.

Quite a few prayer stories were written by door-to-door sales people who sold spiritually based books and magazines. In earlier days they were called colporteurs. I was one myself for five hot summers in Utah and Nevada. Those five summers provided the best education I ever received. During them I learned about human relationships, motivation, psychology, persistence, and diversity. "Cold canvassing," I still believe, has to be the hardest kind of selling there can be. It was during those summers that I discovered just how flimsy a structure wealth is.

The Providence of a Tornado

Harold Funk

I was jogging along steadily, speaking now and then to my faithful old horse, who had been a close companion to me on many of my long colporteur journeys. But things seemed weird and unnatural. The quietness of the leaves, the absence of even a breeze, and the intense heat warned me that something was going to happen.

Then I noticed that the clouds were acting peculiarly. They were moving from several directions to a common center, where the mass grew darker and more threatening. Suddenly, three whirling, funnel-shaped projections appeared, hanging down from the dark mass. The two closer to its edge were being drawn rapidly into the one in the center, which almost instantly started whirling earthward. It had become a tornado, and in a few moments its mighty power would be upon me!

Instantly I drew up rein and with frantic haste unhitched my horse and made it as secure as possible in a nearby shack. Then I ran on, looking about for an entrance to the house as I ran. All at once I stumbled over an old plow, which sent me sprawling headfirst upon the ground. Unhurt, I jumped to my feet and discovered just before me a wooden door slanting against the foundation. The cellar—the safest place I could possibly find! I hurried to open it and clambered inside, closing the door over my head as I went down the steps. A quick search through my pockets for a match was rewarded only by a stub, which failed to light. I groped about in the semi-darkness and stumbled over a pile of rubbish in an attempt to reach a dirty window.

Suddenly, out of the darkness behind me came the slam of the cellar door, and I could barely make out a dark form stumbling down the stairway. In its haste, it lost its footing and fell. No sooner did it strike the dirt floor, however, than it scrambled to its feet and turned to stare at me.

In the dim light, I recognized Mr. Thomas Glassford, the rich man of the rural community, at whose home I had called only a few days before. The incident marking our meeting flashed through my mind.

In contrast to our present surroundings of the cobwebbed, odorous, dirt walls of an abandoned cellar, I saw the bright lights of a large reception room into which a servant ushered me. I noticed on the walls a number of beautiful paintings. The artistically arranged furniture was made of a rare old mahogany.

In the far end of this room, the person to whom I wished to speak sat before a large fireplace. He had the appearance of one who felt assured that wealth could adjust all according to his will. He held my card in his hand.

"You certainly have a beautiful home," I remarked as a preface to my canvass.

"Oh, I feel quite at home in it," he answered. "What can I do for you, young man?"

"I came to tell you about immense wealth that can be had merely for the asking," I said.

At that, he became all attention, and I began to outline the simple, wonderful plan of salvation and then swung into the presentation of my book.

He listened for several minutes, then, his face red with anger, he shouted "Stop!" and pointing to the door, added, "Get out! If there were a God, there would be justice in this world! Get out, I tell you!" So, there being evidently nothing else to do, I went.

Now this selfsame man stood before me trembling with fear. I could hear his deep breaths above the thundering outside. He tried to speak, but only choked and stammered. He tried again, and a high, strained voice betrayed his terror. "We're in its path! We'll be killed! Can't we do something?" Then, suddenly recognizing me, he exclaimed, "You're the book agent! Where's your God? Pray to Him! Pray *now*!" Then the intense heat caused him to choke, and his voice was smothered.

The air was thick with the distinctive odor produced when electricity burns metal, and deafening blasts of the thunder came again and again. Then lightning flashed through the dark cellar, and I could see Mr. Glassford clutching his throat.

For the moment I forgot my God and my companion as I thought of an acquaintance who had been torn from his shelter and played with by a mighty twister until most of his bones were broken. He was found later in the crotch of a tree. I also remembered the utter demolition of the homes of friends and the breaking up of families within my circle of acquaintance by the force of similar tornadoes.

My mind thus crazed with fear, I began to look frantically for a place to hide. My body was wet with perspiration. Then suddenly I realized that God must still be in His heaven, that He is a merciful God, and all-powerful, and that I must trust Him for deliverance. As suddenly as I had lost it, I gained my composure, and said calmly, "Let us kneel and ask our God to protect us."

We knelt there on the dusty ground together, and I prayed, asking forgiveness of sins for both myself and my companion, and divine protection from the raging storm. As I finished my prayer, there was a terrific blast of wind, and for a moment the air seemed to be sucked from the cellar. I clutched my throat and struggled for breath. Then I heard Mr. Glassford speaking. He was sobbing as he prayed, but he did not seem to choke.

He began, "O Almighty God, I am not worthy of Your protection! But save me from this demon of nature, and I will never again speak against You. I have a wife and children. They need me. Don't take me from them—I'm not ready to go. O God in heaven, have mercy upon—"

The sound of wood being broken to splinters mingled with thunder and the crashing of trees seemingly directly over us drowned his last words. My head almost burst with pain as I struggled for air.

Then it started to rain, and great torrents blew in through the window I had broken.

"We are saved, we are saved!" shouted my companion. "There *is* a God!"

We dared not leave our musty refuge as yet, so we seated ourselves on boxes in a dry corner and talked. This time Mr. Glassford begged me to tell the Gospel story and asked many questions.

"Here and now I give myself to God," he resolved at last. "I have lost most of my wealth, but what is left is His. I wish to use it as He directs and in His service. My only regret is that I have not known Him as a personal Savior all these wasted years of my life."

As the wind and rain began to calm down, our conversation ended, and we decided to go out and inspect the devastation of the storm. We saw that small trees had been cut off at the ground, great trees were entirely uprooted, and the ground was strewn with debris. Though the shack had been lifted from the ground and pieces of it were scattered hither and yon, my horse was standing where I had left him. At the end of the rope to which it was tied was a large plank, all that was left of the stall.

As I walked toward my horse, I noticed the plow I had stumbled over in my hurry to shelter. The steel beam, which was approximately four inches wide and two inches thick, had been bent to a right angle. But during this process, the plow had hardly been moved. And strange as it may seem, the house still stood.

I walked up to my faithful horse and led him as we started to look for my buggy, though I had little hope of finding it. I then began to wonder how my companion had been driven to seek the same shelter as I, and I inquired.

"This abandoned farm came into my possession recently through a mortgage fore-closure," he explained. "I had my chauffeur leave me here to look things over while he went on to town to do an errand. I saw you frantically unhitching your horse and run-ning for the shack and then for the house. I also saw those terrifying black clouds at that moment and began running for the cellar entrance that I had seen you enter. Before I reached it, I knew we must be directly in the path of the cyclone. I realize that it is only by the grace of a forgiving God that I am alive at this moment."

We found my buggy in the same place in which I had left it, but it was lying on its back, and all four wheels were bent in at the axles, making it appear like a folded baby car-riage. It was impossible to travel in this wreckage; so we collected those of my books that were unharmed, having been well pro-tected by canvas, and both of us mounted my horse, and we set out for a farmhouse about a mile down the road. This had been well out of the path of the storm, and we were made welcome. After we had told our story, I was able to sell several books. The people were very kind, and fitted me with a buggy so I could continue my canvassing in that territory.

Mr. Glassford went back to his beautiful home a changed man, and he was a humble, faithful servant of the heavenly King to the last day of his life. ❧

Prayer in Extremity

John Van Ess

Truly God has a way of reaching His children wherever in the world they happen to reside, and whatever the religion to which they pledge their allegiance. Much of religion is, of course, an accident of birth (in most cases tied to the culture one grows up in).

In an article in the *Missionary Review of the World* of October 1913, under the title, "God's Hand as I Saw It in Arabia," John Van Ess, a missionary of the Lutheran Church, tells how deliverance came to him at a moment of peril as he called on God for help.

In 1910, the tribesmen of the Mesopotamian border, by the junction of the Tigris and the Euphrates, were in conflict with Turkish forces. All was tumult and violence in the district. In journeying from Baghdad to his mission station at Nasiriyeh, southward on the Euphrates, Mr. Van Ess found himself in the hands of men evidently intent on killing and robbing him. They wanted to push him on out of their village, but he had insisted on resting for a time in a hut, with the tribesmen waiting outside. He says,

My cook, who was an Arab, had . . . been sitting outside of the hut listening to the conversation among the tribesmen. Partly to give him something to eat, and mostly to hear what he had heard, I called him in. He understood the situation at once, and sat with his back to the door. Then he broke a piece of the bread, and as he raised it to his mouth, he whispered, "By no means leave the hut, for they have planned to shoot us." Toward three o'clock in the afternoon, they became impatient at our stubbornness, and one of their number began to insult me. This was a signal for the rest. In my extremity I lifted my heart to God, and asked Him to show His face.

Scarcely had the petition left my

heart when a shadow darkened the doorway, and a tall Arab, with face closely muffled, entered the hut. He was a member of the tribe, and a man of some consequence, judging by the respect they paid him. He at once spied me sitting in the corner, looked me over a minute or two, and then came forward and said: "Salaam, sahib, I am glad to see you here."

I must have looked puzzled, for he unmuffled his face, and said: "I was a patient in your hospital at Busrah two years ago. Your doctor there performed an operation on me, and I was a guest in your hospital for thirty days. Welcome to our camp." Then he began to tell the Arabs of our work at Busrah, and of how he was fed and nursed and healed. He added: "O Arabs, do these men no harm. They and their companions are disciples of Isa el Messiah. They fear Allah, and are our best friends."

A deep silence fell on those assembled, and I thanked God for His great deliverance. Then I told them I wanted to reach Nasiriyeh if possible before sunset. Mohammed at once took his rifle and cartridge belt; and with him and five other Arabs we rode until we reached a ditch about half a mile outside of Nasiriyeh. They dared not enter, for fear of the soldiers, but said they would hide in a ditch, and see that I reached the Turkish line in safety. Just as I turned the corner to enter the town, I looked back, and there stood those six Arabs, faithful to their word. They waved their rifles in farewell, and thus I rode into the town and into safety.

No wonder the missionary says that he saw God's hand in Arabia. In many other perils on this journey he was sensible of the Lord's protecting care over him; but of the crisis in the experience he could truly say with the psalmist, "I cried unto the Lord with my voice, and He heard me." ❧

*I*n the midst of terrible pain, to "just let go" can seem like the logical thing to do—especially when energy to fight a severe malady is in short supply.

How is it possible to resist such a temptation?

Choose Life

Kathleen Ruckman

Kathleen Ruckman has become a cherished friend over the years. This is the third story bearing her name that we have anthologized.

"Kathleen," the doctor said, leaning over me with a gentle but concerned expression on his face, "we just got your husband's permission. We've done all we can here at Sacred Heart. We're going to airlift you to Portland's university hospital. They have the best heart transplant facility in the Northwest."

Best heart transplant facility? I thought, shocked at the statement. Healthy at age forty-three, I had never had heart problems of any kind.

A dark gray sky and a steady Oregon rain matched the mood of the early morning. Attached to eight machines with wires and tubes, I struggled for air. Beeping monitors, concerned nurses running in and out, and even the smells of the sickroom made me feel trapped and helpless. I couldn't talk to the people around me because of my oxygen mask, but I was able to talk to God over and over again in my heart.

It had all begun with flu-like symptoms just a few days earlier. Now, in third-degree heart failure, I couldn't believe what the doctor had said. A probable diagnosis was made, which would be confirmed in Portland: severe, acute viral myocarditis. In other words, a virus had viciously attacked my entire heart muscle.

A pulmonary physician came to drain my lungs, the worst of all my procedures. I hung off the edge of the bed, praying for God to help me get through it. Due to the heart failure, my lungs filled up with fluid, and my kidneys showed signs of failure as well.

That morning, my husband, Tom, got our kindergartner off to the neighbor's house and then made it to the hospital as final flight arrangements were made. Tom was told by the physician that at two hundred pounds, he weighed too much to make the flight with me.

"I'm too fat, Kathy," Tom said tenderly with a weak smile. Actually, Tom isn't fat; he's tall and strong. But he made me smile too.

"I'll drive the kids up in the van, and I'll see you in Portland," Tom said, his voice breaking. Then he left for four different schools to pick up the kids. Shortly afterwards, the doctor came in with bad news about the weather. "Kathleen," he said, "conditions are too poor for a helicopter. We're going to transport you by ambulance to the Eugene airport, where a medical airplane will be waiting. When you get to Portland, an ambulance will take you to Oregon Health Sciences University Hospital. You'll have lots of good care on the flight."

Little did I know that the physicians weren't sure I'd even survive the flight. They kept this information from Tom and me until the crisis was past.

Alone in my room, I felt the presence of God and yearned intensely for heaven. Suddenly, I thought of my mother, who had died almost exactly two years earlier, right around Easter. It seemed she was standing to my right. I felt close to her, and it was then that I almost let go.

Clinging to life was difficult. It would have been easier to let go. I believe in heaven, and I believe in eternal life with God. My mother loved Jesus, and I missed her presence in my life. If I let go, I would awaken in the kingdom. I would be with my mother again—and with Jesus forever.

My yearning for my mother seemed to intensify as my faintness and physical weakness worsened. I kept thinking of her—when out of the blue, words Moses had spoken, or at least written, interrupted my thoughts. They were words of Scripture that I hadn't read for at least the past two years: "I have set before you life and death, blessings and curses. Choose life so that you and your descendants may live" (Deuteronomy 30:19, NRSV).

Then, just as swiftly as the Scripture had come, thoughts of Tom and our children came to my mind. For some reason, I pictured them off to the left. Still thinking of my mom, but now thinking of my family too, I knew what God was asking me to do. I made a conscious decision, right then and there, not to think of my mother until much later. I would focus on Tom and the children. I would not let go. I would choose life.

I had begun reading the Bible at age eleven, when I first dedicated my life to God. From that day on, a hunger for the Bible stirred in my soul. The Scriptures became God's love letter to me, and I found myself applying the wisdom and principles of the Bible to my everyday life. Years later, in my hospital room, when the words *choose life* came to my memory, I knew the Holy Spirit had spoken to me through the written Word I had loved since childhood.

The paramedics came bringing a sheet. As they prepared me for the flight, I felt like a mummy, wrapped from head to toe. When they transferred me from the stretcher to the ambulance, the cold March wind whipped against me. The sheet was too thin, and I shivered as my teeth chattered and raindrops fell on my face. But I would choose life—and cling to life. Most importantly, I would cling to God, who already knew the outcome.

By Easter weekend, four days later, my heart had improved enough that the team of heart failure specialists decided against the transplant. "Kathleen," one cardiologist said, "you should see the exclamation marks in your file!"

Given a 4 to 10 percent chance to live on the day of my flight, I survived with no permanent heart damage. I was named "The Miracle Patient" at the hospital and "The Easter Miracle" at my church.

My physicians released me two weeks after I made the unexpected turnaround, ordering me to rest for several months and to be monitored by a cardiologist for one year.

Tom drove me home from the university hospital. My children welcomed me at the door, and I hugged all four of them, one by one. I realized the extent of it all when I knelt down to hug our kindergartner, who smiled with her baby teeth a grin so big that it melted my heart. I had made it home again.

God's hand had interrupted human events, because it was simply not my time. God reminded me to *choose life,* and now, all these years later, each day is a gift. ❧

SECTION FOUR

"I also tell you this: if two of you agree
here on earth concerning anything you ask,
my Father in heaven will do it for you.
For where two or three gather together
as my followers, I am there among them."
—Matthew 18:19, 20, NLT

"Fittingly, some of the most articulate prayers
come from the mouths of children."
—Yancey, page 320

*E*ven though this is such a simple little story, in its quiet way it implored me to let it crawl into this book.

NUMBER TWO

Author Unknown

It all began with little Bobby's grandmother falling downstairs and breaking her leg. Mrs. Batty went to a church that neglected prayer to such a degree that only she and the minister, Mr. Alister, were usually present at the weekly meeting for prayer.

When the old lady found herself in bed with a broken leg on the day of the prayer meeting, she was in great distress. Her little grandson was having supper with her, and he overheard her telling her neighbor about it.

"You see," said Mrs. Batty, "I'm number two. You know the Bible says, 'Where two or three are gathered together in My name, there am I in the midst of them.' There's just me and the minister, and the Lord comes. And now there'll be no number two."

Bobby crept out of the room, reached up to the peg for his overcoat, and struggled into it, saying to himself, *The minister won't be alone tonight. I'll go and say prayers with him. And then God will come too.*

Presently, having escaped from the house, he was marching bravely up the dark street. An old farmer, Peter Quirls, met him and wanted to know what he was doing out so late.

"Granny's broke her leg," said Bobby, "and I'm going to say my prayers with the minister. I'm number two, and if I go, the Lord'll come." And on he went.

The minister was in his church, waiting for his people to come to prayer. Presently in came little Bobby.

"What do you want, my little man?" asked Mr. Alister.

"Please, Granny's broke her leg and can't come," was the reply. Then the little voice went on: "Please, is God here? I 'spect He'll come now that He sees me here."

The minister stared.

"Granny says He promised that if there were two, He would come; and I'm number two instead of Granny."

"Have you come to pray with me, Bobby?"

asked the minister, laying his hand very tenderly on the flaxen, curly head.

Bobby nodded. "I can say my prayers, an' you can say yours, an' then the Lord won't go away disappointed 'cause nobody wanted to speak to Him."

The minister knelt down, and so did Bobby, and so did old Peter Quirls, who had followed Bobby and was hiding at the rear of the church. Such a wonderful prayer the minister prayed. It was as though he felt God was there. And Bobby prayed—his little prayers that he loved so much.

This was too much for Peter Quirls, who came stumbling awkwardly up the aisle and offered his prayer, in broken tones, with the others.

When they arose from their knees, he turned to the minister. "You'll never see me absent from prayer meeting again, minister!" he said huskily and hurried away.

And so Bobby saved the prayer meeting, for Peter Quirls told everybody, and they all began to feel ashamed and began to attend the meeting. How pleased Bobby's granny was, and how pleased God must have been! ❧

GOD, THE SHERIFF'S CAR, AND THE FROZEN MEAT

Steve Hamilton

My cousin Steve Hamilton grew up on a ranch in California's San Joaquin Valley. This particular story was one he could never forget. Years later, after dialoguing with the Vasconcellos family, he wrote it out for me.

It just had to be part of this collection. (And this has to be the longest title of a story I've ever anthologized!)

It was 1944, and our country was in the midst of World War II. The men and women who worked in the agricultural industries were considered strategic workers because they provided the food and other supplies that kept everyone—including our armed forces—alive, healthy, and able to fight.

Back then, very few people had refrigerators with freezing compartments. Instead, there were cold storage lockers—large buildings that were divided into cubicles that resembled big baskets with doors on them. People could rent these frozen food lockers and keep the food they wanted to preserve until they needed it. These cold storage buildings were cold—about –20 degrees; but if you made your trip into one brief, you didn't have to wear a jacket.

On a warm California evening, Joe Vascon-cellos went to the building where his family's food was stored to get what they would need the next day. He didn't expect to be there long, so he wore just a T-shirt and a pair of pants.

As Joe was walking down the aisle toward the place where his family's food was kept, all the lights in the building went out and the foot-thick insulated door slammed shut, as did the door to the office. Then all was dark and silent.

"Hey! I'm still in here!" Joe called out. And then, suddenly realizing his danger, he stumbled his way through the darkness toward the doors, shouting at the top of his lungs: "Help me! Let me out!" But the building remained deathly quiet.

In the total darkness, Joe felt along the walls for ladders, tools—anything he might use to break through the doors. He thought surely there must be someone left in the office.

The employees wouldn't have left him in there; that they'd probably be back! And then panic overcame him. He felt around until he found the heavy metal door, and then he started banging on it. He pounded his fists on that door until the skin on his knuckles broke open and blood started oozing out. However, the physical damage didn't deter him; he pounded and screamed all the more.

Soon Joe found the frozen metal door again. Now, his blood froze to his hands, arms, and everything else that touched it, and when Joe ripped himself away, some of his flesh ripped off his hands. It was frozen to the spot.

When about twenty minutes had passed, the intense cold began to have an impact beyond mere discomfort. His thinking became fuzzy; his lungs felt as if they were on fire; his eyes were freezing shut; his ears were numb; and all bodily functions were slowing. The one consolation he had was that his eyes adjusted a bit to the darkness, and he could see his way around better.

Joe now saw that there were two tiny windows at the very top of the twelve-foot wall on the Lander Avenue side of the building. And while he was feeling his way along the wall, his fingers bumped into a light switch. When he turned it on, he could see that each window was about a foot tall and eighteen inches wide.

With Joe's newly found sight, he surveyed the entire big room, looking for a ladder and some tools. But he didn't find either.

Then, suddenly, he had an idea. If he threw chunks of frozen food at the windows, he might be able to break one. His hope was that the broken glass and frozen food would fall onto Lander Avenue, and someone there would notice it.

Joe began to follow this strategy, and after several tries, he was successful. One of the packages of meat he tossed went through one of those windows. Joe's success gave him a glimmer of hope and got him thinking again. He decided that to conserve his energy, he'd stop throwing things till he heard a car stop on the street outside the building. When he did, he'd start yelling and throwing things to catch their attention. So he stopped throwing those packages of food, but nobody came.

Finally, in desperation, Joe prayed, "God, can You help me?" Then he clumsily grabbed a package of frozen meat from his locker and headed toward a window. By that time his hands were so cold and stiff that he couldn't even feel the package. He heaved it with all his strength anyway—and the package flew through the dead center of the window, never touching a thing. Then Joe thought he heard a car stop; so, desperately, he began yelling again, "*Please help me! Please help me get out!*"

A sheriff's deputy, done patrolling for the day, had noticed some debris near the building—the packages of food that Joe had thrown through the window. When the deputy slowed to get a better look, a package of frozen meat flew out the window, bounced off the pavement, and hit his door with an awful thud.

The deputy turned on his flashers and got out of his car to figure out what was going on. That enabled him to hear Joe's faint cry for help.

The deputy sprang into action immediately. He jumped into his car and drove into the parking area near the entrance to the building, his siren screaming. He left it on as he scrambled out of the car, and the commotion that followed was ear-splitting and hard to describe. Remember, we were at war, and everyone's nerves were on edge. Every farmer, dairyman, and mechanic within earshot came running to the building to see if they could help. The deputy called out, "Put away your guns, guys, and get some tools. We've got to rescue someone who's inside!" Those who had brought their tools went to work, and the door was demolished in seconds.

By the time they got Joe out, though, he had fainted. And covered with blood from head to toe as he was, for a while no one recognized him. But then one of the bystanders looked in Joe's car and discovered his identity. Then the people there realized that they had rescued one of the most well-known men in Turlock, California: Joe Vasconcellos. Quickly but carefully they laid him on the backseat of the patrol car with a couple of men, one on each side, to hold him as the car, with siren blaring, headed to the hospital a few blocks away.

Joe survived, but that's only part of the story.

The Vasconcelloses and their extended family were important parts of our community. They had emigrated from the Azores, islands off the coast of Portugal. Most of these immigrants were dairymen and cattlemen, and they were the backbone of our thriving economy. However, Joe wasn't a farmer. No, he was the man who helped us buy and sell all of our livestock and equipment. He was the best-known auctioneer in the San Joaquin Valley.

I was only six years old when this happened, but I had already been going with my dad to the auction every Tuesday, and I knew the high regard Dad had for Joe.

At least three or four weeks passed before Joe returned to the auction. Dad and I were there when he showed up again—and so were several hundred others who came to welcome him back!

The auction arena at the Turlock Sales Yard held only about 150 people, but that day at least twice that many squeezed in—the place was packed. There were even people in the ring—the family that owned the company, all of their twenty or thirty employees, the deputy who had rescued Joe, several of the Vasconcellos family, and Joe's two assistants, who were sitting up in the auctioneer's booth. Joe's arms and hands were still covered with bandages, and he was wearing a pair of fleece-lined leather mittens.

When Joe climbed the stairs that led to his seat high above everyone else, he stood silently for a moment. He then said, "Will everyone please stand with me? And please remove your hats!" He then bowed his head and prayed: "God, thank You that we can—all—be here this morning. Help us to do what is right today. Thank You for having the sheriff's deputy in the right place at the right time! And God, thank You for helping me hit the sheriff's car with the frozen package of meat! Amen."

Then all the people in the ring hurried out through the livestock exit gate—all except the ringmaster, who stayed in the ring to help take bids and to help get the cattle out of the ring after the sale.

Then, with no pause, no explanation, and no other comments, Joe sat down and rattled off in his dynamic but intentionally monotone voice, "Bring in the first string of steers. Here we have our first pen of ten steers—they are looking good. Let's start at 25. Do I have 25, 25, 25?"

"Yes," said the ringmaster.

"Now 27, 27, 27. I have 25, now 27, 27, 27. Yes; now 30, 30, 30. I have 27 cents a pound, now 30. Yes. Now 32, 32, 32. I've got 30; now 32, 32, 32. Do I have 32?"

The ringmaster, seeing there was no higher bid, quickly said, "Let 'em go, Joe!"

"Going once. Going twice! Sold," said Joe, and he called out the buyer's name as the ringmaster handed the buyer his slip through the fence separating the ring from the gallery.

"*Next!*" hollered Joe, and out went the ten cattle that were sold, and ten or twelve more entered the ring from the other side.

Joe was back! Dad and I were teary-eyed. That day I learned a lesson that has stayed with me for life. Joe wasn't afraid to stand in front of hundreds of friends and associates and give God *all* the credit! ❧

The most significant and life-changing assignment I have ever given to students (college-age and adult-degree older students) was one that I called "The Nightingale Assignment." It was the one assignment that served to initiate a life-changing epiphany for many who followed the requirements. At the heart of it was the mandate that they experience one hour a day of absolute silence over a period of four to six weeks. During that time they were to read motivational material I provided for them and to think, ponder, conceptualize their future, analyze their past, etc. Most of my college-age students couldn't even remember the last time they had experienced any silence. They just didn't know what to do with it. Thanks be to God, many turned their lives around as they listened to His still small voice.

A FATHER'S PRAYER

Author Unknown

John told me that Phil Land died a few minutes ago, Nannie," said Andrew Bordman, coming into the room where his wife sat sewing.

Andrew Bordman seldom showed emotion, but there was a catch in his voice now. It is not every day that one loses one of his closest friends.

"I tremble for young Phil," sighed Mrs. Bordman. "Wild as he's been with his father here to restrain him, what will he come to without him? Poor Sara won't be able to do anything with him."

"I hope Philip left a will, tying up his property so the boy can't run through it all. All that money just now would only be an added weight to pull him down, I fear . . . "

It was more than a week later that Andrew Bordman again stood by the fire in the room in which his wife sat sewing.

"I witnessed the reading of Philip's will a few minutes ago, Nannie," he said.

"Did he have things fixed so Phil can't spend all he's got?"

"No! It was given him in full. The property was divided equally between Sara and young Phil. She's to have the home place and the money in the bank. Phil gets the rest of his father's properties."

Mrs. Bordman shook her head. "It isn't best, I'm afraid, Andrew. Seems as if it doesn't show Philip Land's good judgment. With young Phil not yet twenty-one, looks like he might have had it held in trust for him. Has he power to sell?"

Andrew Bordman nodded. "Joe Carey says he heard Phil say not a month ago that if he ever came into possession of his father's land-holdings, he'd turn them into cash pretty quick, and have the time of his life," he added sadly.

Tears came into Mrs. Bordman's kind eyes. "Poor Sara! And he being an only child makes it harder still."

"There was a sealed letter, addressed to Phil, in the envelope with the will," continued Andrew. "I was there when he read it. He looked puzzled at first, and read it again. There couldn't have been more than half a dozen sentences, I judge. When he had finished reading it the second time, he got up and left the room."

The whole community waited for Philip Land, Jr., to begin the process of running through the property he had inherited. There were various guesses as to how long it would take him, but even the most lenient conceded him only a few years. A number laid plans to buy pieces of his land when they would be offered for sale.

But the property wasn't offered for sale immediately. To everyone's surprise, after a time, young Philip began to prepare to cultivate it himself, and it was rumored that he showed signs of having turned over a new leaf. The change was generally attributed to the contents of the letter from his dead father, but no one could be sure, for the boy had not even told his mother what the letter said. . . .

As months and years passed, those who had been at first frankly skeptical half forgot the old waywardness, and gradually Philip Land, Jr., began to fill his father's place in the community.

Many years after the death of his father, when his character seemed firmly established, young Phil sat before his own fireplace one evening, talking with Richard Alexander, an old schoolmate who had come back to the community after a long absence.

"I have never heard what it was that made you turn your life around like you did, Phil. Was it your father's death?"

Philip Land looked into the fire in silence for a moment.

"Yes, and no," he answered presently. "Of course, Father's death was a shock, but I had sunk so low that the first thing I thought about when I knew he was gone was that I would come into all that property—the life I had been leading had gone that far in dulling all my finer sensibilities. When the will was read, I was secretly jubilant over the fact that there were no strings tied to my inheritance.

"In the envelope with the will was a sealed letter addressed to me. I know now that as I opened it I was unconsciously steeling myself against an entreaty from my dead father to change my way of living. This was not what I found. Instead, I saw a single paragraph in my father's writing requesting me, as the last thing I should ever be able to do for him, to go down to Spring Hollow by myself every day for a month and spend thirty minutes there in serious thought.

"You remember Spring Hollow, don't you—about a quarter of a mile east of the house? It was such a secluded spot that my father had used it as a place of retreat when he wished to be alone with God. I had seen him, many and many a time, when business or other worries were heavy upon him, start off in the direction of Spring Hollow. And once, when I was a little fellow, I had come upon him there, on his knees, praying aloud. So the place was full of memories of hm.

"It had been so long since I had thought seriously about anything that I was at first at a loss as to what to think. That first time I went there alone, I spent what seemed a long time in wondering what Father had meant. I looked at my watch. I had been there only five minutes. Then suddenly, my subject for thought was furnished me—I believe now as directly from God as was the ram Abraham found caught in the bushes when his hand was stayed from sacrificing Isaac.

"I heard a crackling of dried branches above the spring, and through the pines in front of me was thrust the repulsively distorted face and bleared eyes of old man Adams. He was half intoxicated, as usual, and had wandered out of his way. With a few silly words to me, he went stumbling on.

"The sight of that reprobate, drink-ruined old man Adams in the spot where every leaf and blade of grass spoke to me of my father formed a contrast that was startling, revolting. I knew that the two men had been boys together, and I had heard Father say that no boy in the country had had brighter prospects than George Adams. What had brought about the change? More forcibly than any amount of talking, this illustration of the outcome of the very kind of life I had been leading was driven home to me. I was afraid—horribly afraid—of myself. Impulsively, I fell on my knees, as I remembered seeing my father do, and prayed aloud to God to give me strength to keep from following in old man Adams's footsteps.

"The next day I came to the spring again, early in the morning this time, for I dared not wait till afternoon, and I prayed to God for strength. I came the next, and the next, until it became a habit with me.

"After a time, people began to notice a change in me, and some few seemed to be beginning to have a little faith in me."

Philip Land ceased speaking and sat looking into the fire in silence. Had he looked at his friend, he would have seen that he was much moved.

Presently, Richard Alexander spoke, an unwonted eagerness in his voice. "Thank you, Phil, for confiding in me. I should not have asked you, perhaps, but I am glad I did. I'm glad you told me, and I'm going to try your plan for myself. It has had such an effect on you that I think it may do something for me. Anyhow, I intend to give it an opportunity to work some change in *my* life. God knows I need it."

Philip Land grasped his friend's hand. "Do it, Rich," he said seriously. "I have never yet come to the point in my life where I feel that I can get along without that quiet time for communing with God each day. Indeed, the older I get, the more I feel the imperative need of it." ❧

*S*omewhere between forty million and sixty million people died during World War I and the terrible Spanish Flu epidemic that followed that war. The chaos that followed resulted in blood flowing like water in Eastern Europe and the Balkans.

Rarely did the editors of The Youth's Instructor *(a Christian magazine for young people) republish stories from the secular press. However, they were so impressed by the first-person story published in the* Pictorial Review *that they made an exception for this story, making it the lead story in their May 1, 1923, issue. Once I read it, I knew it just had to be included in this collection of answer to prayer stories.*

Sophie and Her God

Mark O. Prentiss

It was the night of the third day of the fire. We were standing on the quay, a huddled group of Americans trying to direct the groaning, seething mass of humanity round about us. I had climbed on the chassis of a burned Standard Oil Truck to get out of the mass of people who seemed to be literally pushing us into the sea.

No words can picture the pandemonium, the relentless, hopeless, unremitting effort of the fear-maddened crowd to get somewhere, anywhere, out of the pursuing hell of fire and away from the feared avenging Turk.

One of the bluejackets beside the truck called out, "Mr. Prentiss, give me your hand! They've caught me; I can't get loose and they're going to break my back."

I got down so I could try to pull him out of the maelstrom of human beings. As I gave him my hand I felt another hand, a small one, slip into my other hand. After three days and nights of having your clothes clawed, held, torn even, by humans begging for their lives,

one more or less didn't mean much. And yet there was something so warm and tender, so intensely alive and human, that I turned to find its owner.

There she stood, not over ten or eleven, and, most remarkable of all in that dread scene, with a smile on her face.

I had seen every emotion of sorrow and despair depicted on human features during those three awful days. I was almost stunned. It had been such an eternity of horror that this child's smile seemed like a forgotten bit of the joy of life that I could remember only with a struggle. And then she spoke. And in English! It was almost more than I could bear.

Trying to direct this crowd of despairing people, everywhere a babel of Turkish, Greek, Armenian, and then this child's voice in my own tongue! It seemed like an angel's. But her words were even more surprising. "I'm so glad you are here. I won't be afraid any more, now. *He* said you would come."

It took half an hour to worm the thin little figure out of the pressing mass of humans to a place of comparative safety from trampling feet. Shortly after midnight it was possible to get her through a doorway into comparative quiet and safety.

As I carried the child through the crowd, her words of two hours before repeated themselves: "I won't be afraid any more. *He* said you would come."

"So you were expecting me, were you?"

"Oh, yes. *He* told me."

"*He* told you? Who did?"

"God did."

In all the mixed emotions of the hour I thought I had not heard aright and repeated my question. And in that same casual tone, reporting the conversation of a beloved and intimate comrade, the answer came: "God did."

"You see," she explained, "after I lost Mother and my baby sister I began to be afraid. There were so many people, and if anyone fell they walked on him. And it was cold and dark, and I was hungry and I was scared. So I prayed to God and asked Him to come quickly and help me. But He told me He was awfully busy. There were so many people in trouble who wanted to talk to Him that He couldn't get away, He was so busy. But then He told me He would send somebody, and here you are, and so now I know it's all right!"

It gave me an indescribable thrill.

To a plain businessman used to the ordinary experiences of everyday life, this friendly familiarity with the Divine seemed unreal. The poise and quiet assurance of all being well in the face of uncontrolled fear and anguish all about made the whole incident more amazing. If a man hasn't got a God, he has to respect a little child who has one.

She said her name was Sophie Serafim, and that she had been born in America. A year before, with her family, she had gone back to a little town in Asia Minor. Sophie's migration had changed many things for her, but not her God nor her faith in the "Americano."

As I left her, I promised to be back in a few minutes to take her to a place to sleep; but it was near daylight before the course of events permitted my return. Coming back, I wondered if Sophie would be there or if she would have wandered away. But snuggled up in the doorway, she was waiting.

The sailors who had been assigned to shore duty had just brought a pot of coffee and some food from the destroyer for mess. After having had her breakfast, Sophie asked me if I was ready to start to find her mother. The father, a rich Greek from the interior, had brought his family to Smyrna with the retreating Greek army. Five days before, he had been seized by the Turks. Then the fire had started, and two days later the mother, Sophie, and baby sister had driven down to the quay for safety. In the crowd they had become separated, and the child had been wandering alone for two days and nights. The calm assurance with which Sophie spoke of finding them, as if we had only to walk halfway down the block of a quiet street, brought a choke in my throat, even though I may be considered a fairly hardened realist.

Sophie, with her good English and perfect Greek, could act as interpreter. It was only reasonable to take the child with me. She would be of real assistance to me, and there was no need to bring to her before it was necessary the realization that she would probably never see her family again. As we walked along I tried to tell her of the number of people that were wandering about, and of how difficult it would be, but she only smiled sweetly and said, "But God said you would find them. Don't worry about it. You and God can do anything."

I had never thought of myself coupled with Divinity, but I was to hear the phrase many times in the next week, and to remember it for the rest of my life.

During the morning we covered a mile along the quay through such a mess of desolate humanity as you never saw. Shortly before noon I was amazed to have Sophie pull my sleeve. "There they are, my mother and sister!" And coming toward us I saw a grief-crazed woman carrying a baby, hysterical with joy at this miracle of her regained daughter and the intimate guardianship of an "Americano." It was Sophie who calmed her mother, who explained that God had promised her that He would bring them all together again.

When we had the family, with several hundred other women and children, safely conveyed to a building that was to serve as a refuge until such time as we were able to evacuate them, I was prepared for Sophie's suggestion that her father was next.

I got from Sophie her father's name. Then, at my next interview with Haaki Bey, the Turkish commander, I asked for the man. Haaki Bey ordered someone to look up his name and record. Then, with a guide and with a page to call out the man's name, I was taken down into the bullpen where about five thousand prisoners were confined. There was no answer to our paging, and I went back with disappointed heart to tell Sophie that our efforts had been in vain. For the next three days this was a regular part of my schedule, but to no avail.

Then Sophie came to me with a simple, logical explanation of our failure, which in the stress of events had not occurred to me. She said, "My father may be afraid to answer. He may not know that God has sent you to deliver him. Let me go with you." So down into that mass of humanity we went. They put Sophie up on a platform where she could look over the prisoners, and by some small miracle, considering the number of them and the sameness of their misery, she recognized him.

He was conducted to the commander's office. There we were shown his record and the sentence of death by court-martial. The only reason he had not been executed already was that his turn had not come. Knowing the answer in advance, I begged the commander to deliver this condemned man to me. It was with every appearance of regret that he refused my request. My heart was heavy as I went out to the automobile to report my failure to Sophie. Instead of the despair I had anticipated, Sophie put her hand in mine with her usual smile and said, "Don't you worry. Don't you know that the Turks can't hurt my father? Why, God is bigger than all the Turks! They can't hurt him." And so, ashamed before her faith, I was quiet.

When the military governor arrived, I made another unsuccessful attempt. Finally, Nour-ed-din, the most powerful man of his country next to Mustapha Kemal, arrived in Smyrna. I sought an audience and was received by this great man. I asked him for the prisoner. In return he asked, "Is he an American? A naturalized citizen? Has he any claim upon you?"

I could only answer in the negative. "He is a Greek, the father of a little child who has a God, a real God, Your Excellency. He is not your God, nor is He my God, but He has promised this child that her father shall be saved. Can you arrange it?"

Then Nour-ed-din, by skillful questioning, brought out the whole story. With his hand on his heart he said, "You break my heart. There is no other thing I would refuse you. But this is not an affair of the heart. This is *war*. I have many thousands of Turkish children who will never again see their fathers. It is with a breaking heart that I must refuse you. This man has been sentenced to die. He will be executed tomorrow morning."

"Is that final, Your Excellency?"

"I regret that it must be so."

"I cannot blame you. I have seen the records of the case. You probably have executed ten thousand Greeks and will probably kill another fifty thousand before this is over. This one Greek will mean little to you, but he is everything in the faith of this child. Powerful as you are, Your Excellency, and humble as I am, the time might come when you would need a friend in America. If you can find clemency possible, I can assure you of my appreciation, little as it may mean."

"I must tell you no, though my heart breaks."

So I left him and attempted to comfort

Sophie. It was a chance; it was playing dramatics, if you will. But I had nothing to lose, and I was desperate. He had said he would see what could be done.

The next morning a captain of Turkish infantry with half a dozen soldiers brought John Serafim down to the American refugee house where we were living. At the suggestion of this officer, six sailors of the United States destroyer *Edsall,* under command of Captain Haley Powell, formed a hollow square around Sophie, her mother and father and the baby sister, and escorted them to the quay. Here Turks and Americans stood at full salute as the naval launch carried the party out to the boat that was to take them away. The story had spread among our group, and as the boat left shore we were caught up in the rush of a good American cheer from the ship for Sophie and the proving of her faith.

I thought, naturally, that I had seen the last of Sophie. I stayed in Smyrna about three weeks, then went to Constantinople, and thence to Athens, where we had settled thousands of refugees. The Greek officials there wanted to show some appreciation to America for what had been done. Accordingly they singled me out for a little ceremony. We went out to one of the camps where there were some thirty thousand or forty thousand refugees. When I got out of the automobile, who should run up to me out of the crowd but Sophie! She came up, stood on her tiptoes, and threw her arms around my neck.

I confess I cried. Out of all those weeks of horror it was the first time I had shed a tear. As her arms went around my neck she said, "I knew you'd come today—God said you would!"

"Sophie, what did you say?"

"Why, last night I prayed to God because we haven't had much to eat for three or four days, and the people were getting very hungry and unhappy. They all know about you and asked me to pray to God to send you back; so last night I asked Him, and He said you'd be here today."

Isn't it a paradox that a man must go from a Christian country to Turkey to find a real God—one who functions?

Fortunately, or providentially, American supplies had arrived, and I could once more fulfill Sophie's idea and ideal of God's messenger. As she said good-by she added, "I'll see you in America. I've told God how much I want to go. People are so much happier in America. They think about doing nice things for other people and that makes them happy, too."

May God grant her prayer! ❧

*T*his is a very special story for me because my wife, Connie, has quilted all through our married life. Each quilt painstakingly hand stitched. Each a one-of-a-kind work of art—an heirloom her children would battle almost to the death for.

Indeed, a hand-crafted quilt represents one of the very few creations that are priceless. How could mere money buy sweat, blood, tears, sighs—and time, the elixir of life itself?

THE PRAYER QUILT

Velda Anderson

Grandmother Blum sat rocking gently to and fro in her worn little rocker by the window, waiting for the postman. Every day after she had washed the few dishes she and her daughter used for their breakfast and had made up her bed, pulling the white cotton spread evenly over the blankets and smoothing it with her knotty, work-hardened hands, she would take her place by the front window to wait for the postman.

Perhaps there would be a letter from her oldest daughter, Katie. She always looked for her beloved *Weld-Post,* too. The letters had to be laid aside until someone familiar with English could read them to her, but the *Weld-Post* was printed in German, and Grandma read every word carefully, as if missing one single idea were a crime.

Then came a day when she rocked a bit more nervously as she waited for the mail. Katie hadn't been well. Would she hear from her that day?

Nine-fifteen. The postman, prompt as the sunrise, stepped up on the porch, nodded a greeting to Grandma, and dropped a single postcard into the box. Grandma hurried out to get it. Yes, that round, even writing was Katie's. Oh, if only she could read it! Hannah wouldn't be back from town until noon. That was much too long to wait. Fingering the card nervously, she decided to take it to Mrs. Fisher, who lived next door. She would read it to her.

Grandma threw a gray wool shawl over her shoulders and hurried across to the next house. "I have a card here from my Katie. Will you read it to me?" she asked the kind-faced woman who answered her knock.

"Come in, neighbor. I'll be glad to do that."

Grandma was too excited to sit down, so she stood by the door as her neighbor read:

Dear Mother,
We went to see the doctor yesterday,

and he says that he must operate at once in an attempt to save my life. Pray for me. I cannot bear the thought of leaving my four precious children. I'm going to the hospital Monday, and the doctor will operate on Tuesday. Only God can save me.

Your Katie

Tears were in Grandma's eyes as she choked out a hasty "Thank you" and turned to her own little home. Katie was going to have surgery on Tuesday, and that day was Tuesday. There were four children in a farmhouse far away. Dear God, save that mother!

God had never failed her before, and Grandma was confident that He wouldn't fail her now. She fell on her knees beside her little rocker and prayed as only a God-fearing mother can pray. "Father, if it be Thy will, spare my Katie" was the essence of her petition.

Four children, the oldest thirteen years old, the baby only six, were unusually quiet in their farm home. Mummy was in the hospital. Daddy had gotten up early and driven forty miles to be with Mummy when the doctor operated on her at eight o'clock that morning. The children were still asleep when

he left, but they remembered how old and tired his face had looked at the supper table Monday night.

"Mother's at the hospital," Delmar informed the two little ones. "Mother might not get well. The doctor has to hurt Mother with his sharp knife."

Delmar was a big boy—wasn't an eleven-year-old nearly grown up?—but he couldn't keep that lump out of his throat, even by swallowing hard.

The two little ones began to cry. They didn't want sweet, kind Mummy to be hurt.

Sister had tears in her eyes, too. She was the biggest of all, but she didn't even try to stop crying. She only said, "Boys, we must pray to Jesus. He was a doctor when He was on earth. He can make our mamma well. But we mustn't forget to say, 'If it be Thy will.' "

Four little prayers went up to the kind Father who sees all, knows all, and pities His children.

It was nine-fifteen in the farmhouse.

It was nine-fifteen in the hospital. White-clad nurses rolled a stretcher swiftly along the silent halls to "Death Row." The head nurse shook her head gravely as she read the report and assigned a special.

The woman awaiting surgery was only one

more patient, but the nurse felt a pull at her heartstrings as she helped lift the woman onto a surgical bed. She felt sorry for the tall man with the sad face who stood across the bed from her, waiting for the patient to regain consciousness.

He was the sick one's companion, the father of the four children in the farmhouse, and a faithful Christian. All morning he had prayed silently. He had prayed that the surgeon's hand would be guided during the operation. He prayed now that his beloved wife would be given strength to live. He could never give up praying. His God was a faithful God. He would hear.

Grandma rose from her knees. She thought of her workbox. Her hands were not used to idleness. She must be busy now. There was a roll of woolen scraps in the storeroom. They would make a warm quilt for her Katie.

As her scissors snipped the cloth into pieces of the right size, a tune came to her mind, and she began singing. To be sure, her voice was not clear and young, but her heart was sincere as she sang:

Gott ist die Liebe,
Lasst mich erlosen;
Gott ist die Liebe,

Er liebt auch mich.

Translated, the song is

Our God is love,
And His love will save me;
Our God is love,
And He loves me, too.

And so the prayer quilt was started. Every patch was a prayer and every stitch was faith, binding the prayer into a perfect and beautiful whole.

Day by day Grandma worked on the heavy woolen pieces, stitching and praying, sewing and singing, but always believing that God could save her Katie.

And what of the patient sufferer for whom so many prayers were being offered? Was she a child of God? Yes. She was too ill even to speak, but in her heart she held fast to her faith that the Great Physician could heal her. Well she knew that she was battling with that very real demon—cancer. She felt too the very real need her children had for her. She loved them all, but she thought oftenest of her first-born, her daughter, who was just old enough to need a mother's tender love and care to guide her into womanhood. Only she could give her child that love. "God," she pleaded, "spare my life."

Upon her, too, rested the responsibility of

leading her flock to Jesus and pointing them to His sacrifice. She could not leave this burden to her husband alone. He must win the bread. She must win her children. And so she prayed for life—a life of labor.

Every day the husband and father left his children at home with an aunt and came to the hospital. Every day he waited for the first signs of returning health as his wife lay between life and death. When she took her first food, he rejoiced, and when she actually seemed hungry at the following meal, he thanked his Father above. And from then on Katie gained steadily.

When the doctor said she might go home next week, there was rejoicing in the friendly little farmhouse. Every chair was polished; every speck of dust was cleaned away. Loving hands prepared a warm, cozy bed "for Mother."

Grandma, in her little home, sewed faster. The quilt must be finished. It was a token, a monument, if you please, to answered prayer. Soft, fluffy wool had gone inside to pad it and make it warmer. Dark flannel had made the back, and bright yarn had tufted the warm cover.

Finally the last stitch had been fastened and the thread cut. Lovingly Grandma packed her offering into a box for Hannah to address and mail. Grandma wanted the quilt to greet Katie when she arrived at home.

When the box came to the little farmhouse, the children and Daddy decided that its contents must be taken along to the hospital to keep Mother warm on her trip home. And so the quilt was tucked into the front seat, over Mother's lap, and not a bit of cold reached her.

Tender, loving hands helped her from the car to her bed. She tried bravely to walk, but she could only sink into those strong arms that supported her. Mother was still weak.

When she had been tucked into the bed armed with hot irons and water bottles, she heard the story of the quilt. Each child told about it in his or her own way, and when they were sound asleep in their beds that night, even Father tiptoed into her room and told the story.

"Dearest," she said as she reached for his hand, "is it true that you all love me so much that you prayed for me like that? With God's help I will get well and be faithful to you, to my children, and to God."

And so the quilt was made, and so it was dedicated. It remained as a witness to answered prayer and a reminder of a mother's vow.

Last week I visited that friendly little farmhouse. My mother is there—sweet, smiling, and loving. My father greets me—honest, true, a living example of practical Christianity. Mother has grown older and grayer. Her four children are grown and have left their nest. But they still cherish the memories of loving parents.

We had a good visit. I do not get home often anymore. Mother is dreaming dreams with me now of my own home, helping me make things for it. When she goes shopping, she often chooses little things which she thinks I might use and lays them aside for me.

We made a trip to the low-ceilinged, slanting-walled second story, Mother and I. She was going through her well-filled trunks, showing me the quilts she had made since I was home last, and laughing as she exhibited six fluffy pairs of pillows filled with duck down.

"One pair for each of my children when they marry," she said with a laugh, "and two pairs for our guests to sleep on."

Down at the bottom of the last trunk we came across a dark woolen quilt. Mother lifted it out tenderly.

"Do you remember this?" she asked.

The quilt! It smelled of moth balls, but that couldn't drown the fragrance of answered prayer that it brought to us. Neither of us spoke a word. We sat there, just thinking. The years had passed, but the quilt marked an important event in our lives. It marked the triumph of prayer.

" 'The effectual fervent prayer of a righteous man availeth much,' " quoted Mother, and we folded the quilt and replaced it in the trunk.

Grandma still lives. She is too old to make quilts now but she still sits in her worn little rocker and waits for the postman and a letter from Katie. She still sings in her quavering voice "*Gott ist die Liebe,*" and her faith is as strong as it was when she prayed for her Katie and pieced the quilt. ❧

mall things: surely the great God of all the universe would be too busy to come up with a way to buy two blue coats for the price of one. That was her dilemma.

THE MIRACLE OF THE TWO BLUE COATS

B. Lyn Behrens

Some years ago, Dr. Lyn Behrens, then president of Loma Linda University, sent me this remarkable story.

It was cold, and getting colder by the day. Each morning the windshield of the car was frosted over. At sunset the little puddles in the parking lot of the supermarket turned to ice. Our move from sunny Southern California to Denver in the summer of 1981 had been relatively smooth. But as the leaves turned golden in the fall, it was clear that our two growing daughters would need heavy clothing for the Colorado winter. We were unprepared.

My hectic sabbatical study-and-work schedule didn't allow me the luxury of crafting garments for them, so we made multiple brief excursions to the shopping malls looking for coats for the girls. Each time we began with enthusiasm. Each time we returned with growing frustration—we couldn't find anything that fit both them and the extremely tight family budget.

Then the snow began to fall, and I could delay no longer. So we left home early Sunday afternoon and drove to a Kmart south of the city. There in the children's clothing were the perfect all-weather coats—sky blue in color, lined with removable flannel, and just one of each of the sizes my girls needed. But then I glanced at the price tag, and my relief turned to total frustration. Both girls needed coats, but I couldn't afford more than one.

An exhaustive search revealed no other options. Near tears, we drove to the local Target store. But that was no help—absolutely nothing there fit.

Our failure to find what we needed at a price we could afford renewed a dialogue that had begun months before. Then, we had sought God's leading in this career change. Now the reality of our changed circumstances was starkly evident in many ways. Nagging uncertainty mushroomed suddenly into a menacing cloud of doubt. *What should I do,*

Lord? I prayed. *This isn't a want; this truly is a need!*

My inner dialogue moved beyond the need for coats to the larger issue. *God, was it really Your will that we come to the Mile-High City? Did I want to come to this research center so badly that I misread Your leading?*

On the way home we passed the Kmart again. On an impulse I swung the car into the parking lot. The girls chided me for the useless detour. We sat in the car and talked to God about our dilemma. In spite of scanty resources, we had continued to pay a faithful tithe. We claimed God's promise in Malachi 3:10, 11. We wondered what God could and would do for us.

As we passed through the double doors into the store, a voice on the speaker system announced a "new special" in the children's department. It took just seconds to find the flashing blue light. There was only one item of clothing on sale—the very coats we had selected two hours previously!

We heard a voice proclaim, "Two coats for the price of one!"

The garments still hung exactly as we had left them. Grabbing them, we raced to the checkout line. Even the cashier was amazed by our bargain. By the time our purchase was completed, the sale was over! In the space of five minutes our dilemma was solved. We marveled at God's amazing providence and incredible timing.

Through the intervening years the "miracle of the two blue coats" has been a source of reassurance, comfort, and courage. In times of personal and professional perplexity the story reminds me that God knows the details of my life and times. ❧

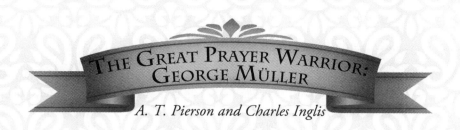

THE GREAT PRAYER WARRIOR: GEORGE MÜLLER

A. T. Pierson and Charles Inglis

Were George Müller's life not so well documented, one would say it was all a fabrication; too improbable to be true. Philip Yancey notes that Müller claimed fifty thousand answers to prayer in his storied ministry. Because of this, one thing was certain: his story had to be included in this book!

An obscure pastor in the west of England was distressed by the general lack of faith in God. "I longed," he said, "to have something to point to as a visible proof that our God and Father is the same faithful God as ever He was, as willing as ever to prove Himself to be the living God."

Praying for guidance in the matter, the pastor was led to establish the work that grew into the great Bristol orphanages. The enterprise truly was, as George Müller desired it to be, a testimony to the living God, who hears prayer and does things on earth.

That this might be evident to all, Müller considered it fundamental in the purpose that neither he nor his fellow workers should ask help of any man, but only of the Lord, in prayer. His thought was: "Now if I, a poor man, simply by prayer and faith obtained, without asking any individual, the means for establishing and carrying on an orphan house, there would be something that, with the Lord's blessing, might be instrumental in strengthening the faith of the children of God, besides being a testimony to the consciences of the unconverted of the reality of the things of God."

The work began in 1835. As it grew from year to year, George Müller's journal traced the record of daily dependence on God. Again and again, with no supplies for the next meal, the need was urged before God in prayer, and the help came. The entry in his journal for December 1, 1842, reports ninety-six orphans in the homes, and a shortage of supplies and money. "We were unable to take in the usual quantity of bread," reads the record.

"It may be asked," wrote Müller here, "Why do you not take the bread on credit?" And then he tells why he considered it essential that there should be no borrowing in that particular enterprise, no taking of goods on credit. He says:

> The chief and primary object of the work was not the temporal welfare of the children, nor even their spiritual welfare, blessed and glorious as it is, and much as, through grace, we seek after it and pray for it; but the first and primary object of the work was to show before the whole world and the whole church of Christ that even in these last evil days the living God is ready to prove Himself as the living God by being ever willing to help, succor, comfort, and answer the prayers of those who trust in Him. . . .
>
> From the beginning, when God put this service into my heart, I had anticipated trials and straits; but knowing, as I did, the heart of God, through the experience of several years previously, I also knew that He would listen to the prayers of His child who trusts in Him, and that He would not leave him in the hour of need, but listen to his prayers and deliver him out of the difficulty;

and that then, this being made known in print for the benefit of both believers and unbelievers, others would be led to trust in the Lord.

> We discern, therefore, more and more clearly that it is for the church's benefit that we are put into these straits; and if therefore in the hour of need we were to take goods on credit, the first and primary object of the work would be completely frustrated, and no heart would be further strengthened to trust in God; nor would there be any longer that manifestation of the special and particular providence of God which has hitherto been so abundantly shown through this work, even in the eyes of unbelievers, whereby they have been led to see that there is, after all, reality in the things of God.

Müller never laid down his own method as the rule for others. He felt only that, with the special call that he had to let the work bear witness to God's daily oversight and faithful providence, he must never assume the burden himself, but must wait on God, going only so far as the Lord made a way. And day by day the Lord vindicated his faith in a wonderful manner.

At last the time came for enlargement, and a building fund for new orphanages, on their own ground, began to come in. Of his experience in securing the land where the great institution was finally placed, on Ashley Down, near Bristol, Mr. Müller says in his journal for the year 1846:

February 4. This evening I called on the owner of the land on Ashleydown, about which I had heard on the second, but he was not at home. As I, however, had been informed that I should find him at his house of business, I went there, but did not find him there either, as he had just before left. I might have called again at his residence at a later hour, having been informed by one of his servants that he would be sure to be at home about eight o'clock; but I did not do so, judging that there was the hand of God in my not finding him at either place; and I judged it best, therefore, not to force the matter, but to "let patience have her perfect work."

February 5. Saw this morning the owner of the land. He told me that he awoke at three o'clock this morning and could not sleep again till five. While he was thus lying awake, his mind was all the time occupied about the piece of land respecting which inquiry had been made of him for the building of an orphan house, at my

request; and he determined with himself that, if I should apply for it, he would not only let me have it, but for one hundred and twenty pounds per acre instead of two hundred pounds, the price which he had previously asked for it. How good is the Lord! . . . Observe the hand of God in my not finding the owner at home last evening. The Lord meant to speak to His servant first about this matter during a sleepless night, and to lead him fully to decide before I had seen him.

As the orphanages filled up till more than two thousand children were being cared for at a time, still it was a work of daily waiting on the Lord for supplies. Day after day closed with no balance in hand, but with each day's absolute necessities met. While the Lord supplied their needs so wondrously, Müller was an economist, saving the littles conscientiously. He felt that only so could he expect God to hear and answer.

Mr. Müller was drawn to pray also for help for foreign missionaries in that time of missionary expansion in far lands; and many gifts were sent him for this work, and for Bible distribution. He says of the help sent to missionaries: "It has frequently, yea, almost always, so happened that the assistance which God has allowed me to send to such brethren has come to them at a time of great need. Sometimes they have no money at all left. Sometimes even their last provisions were almost consumed when I have sent them supplies."

The well-known English evangelist Mr. Charles Inglis whose absolute veracity no one in Great Britain would for a moment question, once told a story that he heard direct from the captain of a steamship on the Liverpool-Canadian service, with whom he crossed the Atlantic. . . . It concerned the captain's experience with George Müller, of the Bristol orphanages.

The sea captain spoken of told his story to Mr. Inglis as the ship was creeping slowly through a fog off the Banks of Newfoundland. Mr. Inglis said that the captain was one of the most devoted Christians he ever knew. The captain said:

Mr. Inglis, the last time I crossed here, five weeks ago, one of the most extraordinary things happened, and it has completely revolutionized the whole of my Christian life. Up to that time I was one of your ordinary Christians.

We had a man of God on board, George Müller, of Bristol. I had been on that bridge for twenty-two hours and never left it. I was startled by someone tapping me on the shoulder. It was George Müller. "Captain," he said, "I have come to tell you that I must be in Quebec on Saturday afternoon." This was Wednesday.

"It is impossible," I said.

"I have never broken an engagement for fifty-seven years."

"I would willingly help you. How can I? I am helpless."

"Let us go down to the chartroom and pray."

I never heard of such a thing. "Mr. Müller," I said, "do you know how dense this fog is?"

"No," he replied, "my eye is not on the density of the fog, but on the living God, who controls every circumstance of my life."

He went down on his knees, and he prayed one of the most simple prayers. I muttered to myself: "That would suit a children's class, where the children were not more than eight or nine years of age." The burden of his prayer was something like this: "O Lord, if it is consistent with Thy will, please remove this fog in five minutes. You know the engagement you made for me in Quebec for Saturday. I believe it is your will."

When he had finished, I was going to pray; but he put his hand on my shoulder and told me not to pray.

"First, you do not believe He will; and, second, I believe He has, and there is no need whatever for you to pray about it." I looked at him, and George Müller said this: "Captain, I have known my Lord for fifty-seven years, and there has never been a single day that I have failed to gain an audience with the King. Get up, captain, and open the door, and you will find the fog is gone." I got up, and the fog was gone!

The lesson is lost if it suggests that Müller's faith enabled him to ask strange things and receive the answer. He didn't make a practice of praying concerning weather conditions. This was the one such occasion, doubtless, in his long life of faith. The lesson is that God does open the right way before faith; and He may, on occasions, make known to His children that it is according to His will that definite request be made for the removal of barriers and the opening of ways where ordinary means fall short and human resource fails.

In summary of this man's life, it appears that Müller, a poor man, had in sixty years been enabled—

"1. To build five of the largest orphanages in the world, in which over ten thousand children had been cared for.

"2. To give to school work over half a million dollars.

"3. To circulate nearly two million Bibles and portions, and three million books and tracts.

"4. To give over a million and a quarter dollars in aid of missionary work in various lands.

"5. Altogether, in the sixty years, this man, without personal resources, who had less than three hundred dollars in money when he died, had had put into his hands to distribute about seven million five hundred thousand dollars."

Truly the Lord helped George Müller to leave the witness, according to his desire, that God is the living God. ❧

SECTION FIVE

"Keep on asking, and you will receive what
you ask for. Keep on seeking, and you will find.
Keep on knocking, and the door will be opened
to you. For everyone who asks, receives.
Everyone who seeks, finds. And to everyone
who knocks, the door will be opened."
—Matthew 7:7, 8, NLT

"Prayer offers an opportunity for God to remodel
us, to chisel marble like a sculptor, touch up colors
like an artist, edit words like a writer. The work
continues until death, never perfected in this life."
—Yancey, page 154

*B*ack in the 1890s, Canada's vast Northwest Territories were very sparsely settled. The life of those who lived there was truly frontier life, and children were trusted with more responsibilities than would be true today. I couldn't help being deeply moved by this story. Truly, God preserved Pearly's life again and again during the ordeal.

THE RUGGED LAND

Juanita Tyson-Flyn

Pearly stopped short in the rutted wagon road as the realization came upon her that she was lost. Her blue-gray eyes opened wide as she frantically searched her surroundings for a familiar spot on the landscape, but it was all the same—low, rolling country covered with prairie grass. Here and there were clumps of shrubs and stands of trees that seemed to hide something from the bewildered child. She ran back and forth trying to see just beyond. Surely there would be something to help her back onto the right path.

But there was nothing. Just more undulating grass as far as the eye could see. There was no doubt about it, Pearly Hallberg was lost, and being lost brought awful feelings to a nine-year-old girl.

Northwest Territories had just been opened up to settlers who weren't afraid of hardships, to those willing to put in long hours of labor on the virgin soil, to those willing to suffer privations and the great solitude of a new land. It was to such a place that Pearly had come two years earlier with her parents and brothers and sisters.

Her father and the two oldest brothers came to the new land first. Of the hardships and trials that come to every pioneer, they had their share and faced them bravely. They staked out a homestead in the Ross Creek District and cleared a bit of land on which to build a rude log cabin to serve the family needs until larger and finer accommodations could be built. Their hands became hard and calloused and many a tear of frustrated fury was shed by the boys as they taxed their strength on the unyielding growth of centuries. Their father—with his quiet Swedish philosophy, a twinkle in his blue eyes, a toss of his shaggy, already white hair, and perseverance—plied his strength with his sons, and together they conquered the land.

By the time the geese were flying south that first year, a neat cabin stood in the clearing with smoke pouring a welcome from the sod chimney. The open windows invited in flies and mosquitoes, but the men inside whistled as they laid wide, smooth boards down to form the floor in the large living room. Already the kitchen was finished, as was the bedroom off the living room. The upstairs was just a loft reached by a ladder nailed firmly to the wall opposite the living room fireplace. Mother would bring calico for curtains to partition the big room, half for the girls and half for the boys.

Only a few more days remained until Father Hallberg would hitch the team of horses to the big lumber wagon and start the forty-mile trip to Fort Edmonton to meet Mother and the younger children, who had waited behind in Fruitland, Washington. In Fort Edmonton, Father would buy panes of glass for the windows of the cabin and stock up on the provisions they needed for the winter months ahead. Before they made that trip, though, the floor had to be finished and the cabin well banked with sod to keep out the furious winds and the snow.

When Mother arrived, she set to work at the task of housekeeping in her new home. Along with her regular work of carding wool, spinning, weaving, and dressmaking—not to mention churning, baking, cooking, and washing—she did what she could to educate her family. She even wrote letters to be published in various leading newspapers in the States, encouraging people to make their home in this country, which challenged every man's mettle.

In the fall of 1894 the Hallbergs were comparatively well settled and had almost a dozen neighbors scattered about them. The common problems of conquering the new land and existing day by day developed the spirit of cooperation and friendly dependence that has made the West famous to this day for its hospitality.

Post offices were few and far between. As time was precious, a system was worked out among the neighbors whereby each week one family would be responsible for the trip to Chipman, the post office, and the mail. The scattered community looked forward to mail day, for it furnished not only newsy circulars and precious letters, but also an opportunity to visit with their neighbors.

Back at home the Hallbergs kept busy gathering the produce of the garden before heavy frosts set in. The parents were especially anxious to get the work done as the days were rapidly growing short and there was a tang in the air already. Soon mail day arrived, but they were so busy preserving the fruits of their garden that it almost seemed there wasn't time to go for their mail.

Then Pearly timidly asked to go. Her eyes pleaded eloquently for her as she rubbed one bare foot over the other. But her mother was dubious. Pearly was only nine. She had been at the Vans' home but once before—she had gone with an older sister on horseback. Now her parents talked long into the night about letting her go.

Upstairs, Pearly crouched by the stovepipe hole listening to the conversation below until Ada, her older sister, almost dragged her to bed. Sleep was out of the question for her in her excitement. Perhaps they would say yes!

"Of course," said her mother, "it would be good for her to play with the Van girls. There hasn't been much time for play. But she is so young to start out alone."

"Well, the snows won't keep off much longer, and we've got to get the garden stuff in before we go to the fort, and to the fort we must go—that's certain," her father commented. "The older children must work harder, but perhaps this once we could spare Pearly."

The morning dawned crisp and bright. But even before dawn the family was up and about. Each child was assigned a chore, and by the time breakfast was on the table, excitement was running high. Who would be the one chosen to fetch the mail?

The children had been taught not to coax, so they sat expectantly around the breakfast table waiting for Father to outline the day's work. At last he looked at Pearly. She hadn't been able to eat a bite because of the excitement within her, and at Father's words she became almost ill with joy.

"You may go for the mail, Pearly," Mr. Hallberg said quietly. "You must return after the lunch hour so as to be back in plenty of time for the evening chores."

"Now, Pearly," coaxed her mother, "do eat your breakfast. There's a long walk ahead of you."

But Pearly couldn't eat. Such a wonderful thing was about to happen—several hours to play with the neighbor children.

Breakfast over, the family gathered for morning prayers. A sense of sustaining power filled the lives of the pioneers. It has helped to make this vast land what it is today.

"Father in heaven," Mr. Hallberg concluded his prayer that morning, "be with our child as she goes into the unknown this morning. Keep her safe throughout the hours she is away. Fit us for Thy kingdom. Amen."

As Mother handed Pearly the small cotton sugar sack in which she was to carry the mail, she patted her and said, "We have to get in the garden stuff so we can go to the Fort, Pa and I. You young ones must have shoes and underwear. The cold won't hold off much longer. Be careful, child."

The little girl with eyes aglow and bare toes she couldn't keep still hugged her mother and went off, skipping down the wagon trail, turning to wave every so often until finally the home place was lost to sight.

What a day! The sun shone benignly on the barefoot girl. A flitting breeze playfully teased her short, straw-colored hair and tickled her neck. She laughed aloud as she skipped along kicking up puffs of dust and now and again flinging her arms wide as if to embrace the whole world.

Then the road forked. That puzzled her a moment. However, shortly she became convinced that she recognized a landmark on the road to the right, and she skipped merrily along again. In a mile or two the road turned into two ruts for a ways and then abruptly stopped. Pearly stopped too. She retraced her steps. How it happened she didn't know, but all at once she knew she was lost.

Terror seized her. She had heard stories about people lost—lost and never found. There were wolves about, she knew, and the panic increased as she ran in one direction and then in another with tears streaming down her dusty face. Eventually, in utter exhaustion she sank to the ground, crying. Oh, why had she wanted to go so much? Why had she been so sure she knew the way? The tears flowed freely between the trembling fingers that covered her face.

Then a meadowlark trilled as it soared into the sky, and she looked up. The meadowlark reminded her of something. It was almost as if it had spoken to her. She brushed the tears from her eyes and got down on her knees and prayed. But when she had finished, terror still filled her heart. Again she prayed. And again, when she stood up, she began to run frantically first one way and then another. Finally in despair she fell on her knees again.

"Please, dear God," she said, "help me to get home. Please protect me and help me." Tears were still streaming down her grimy face.

She remembered the family sitting that morning in a circle in the parlor of their homey log cabin. She remembered her father with the large family Bible open upon his knee, and the psalm he had read. As she recalled the prayer he had offered as he had closed the Book, a feeling of peace came over her. She dried her eyes. All would be well.

All day she walked, stopping occasionally to rest or to pick a tiny prairie flower. She was too young to realize that she was walking in circles.

When the sun hung low in the west and darkness began to send weird shadows across the countryside, she looked around for a place to sleep. A clump of scrub trees solved the problem. Bent branches and fallen leaves made a mattress. Hardly had she sent up her accustomed bedtime prayer than she was asleep.

Soon something awakened her. She sat up in the dark recess of her bower. For a moment a cold shiver crept over her, and then she recognized what she was hearing. The loons were laughing hilariously in a marshy place not far away. In fact, the night air was filled with familiar sounds—the whooping cranes, the honking geese, and the lonely wailing of the coyote.

Pearly lay back on her leafy pillow and went to sleep again. The wind came up, sighing in the trees. She curled up, pulling her chilly feet up under her dress as best she could.

When the sunlight sifted through the trees, caressing her, she awoke. She stretched her aching legs from the cramped position she had been in all night trying to keep warm. Now that the sun was up she would start on her way home, she thought to herself, and crawled from her shelter in the scrubby bushes.

The previous day she had been too excited to think about food, but on this second morning the pangs of hunger made her long for Mother's crushed-wheat porridge with honey and toast with wild Saskatoon berry preserves. Never again would she complain about food if only she could have some right now.

Hour after hour she walked, searching for berries. But the search was in vain. At last, tired and hungry, she found a sheltered spot, pulled the little sugar sack over her aching feet, and with a prayer for help, fell asleep.

At home the Hallberg family was tense with anxiety. When darkness had come and Pearly hadn't returned with the mail, her father had sent the oldest son on horseback to the neighbors, to fetch her. But Abner had returned pale and shaken to tell the startled family that Pearly had never arrived at the neighbors' place with the mail.

Mr. Hallberg and the boys searched the countryside through the night. Neighbors joined in as word spread. By noon, the weary, anxious father decided to send for help. A messenger went on horseback to Fort Saskatchewan, and forty members of the Royal Canadian Mounted Police were sent to join the search.

Pearly awoke before daylight on the third morning. She felt sure she was freezing to death. Every bone in her body ached, and her stomach hurt so much that tears came very near spilling down her cheeks. Before she had very much time to think about her hunger, the overcast morning sky began to sift down wet flakes of snow. They fell faster and faster and soon became large and fluffy, vying with one another to blanket the earth.

Slowly and painfully Pearly crept out from her resting place. Walking might help to warm her cold body.

Finally she found a large spruce tree. The trunk had been snapped about three feet up, and the branches spread out on the ground. She crawled under the prickly branches and found the ground comparatively dry. Putting her feet inside the little sack, she lay down to rest again.

When she awakened she found herself scarcely able to move. Every joint ached, and her hands were swollen and sore. The snow-laden tree had not been able to support all the snow, and as the wind sighed in the bent branches the snow had sifted through onto Pearly.

At last, about noon according to the sun that had come out to melt away the snow, Pearly began once more her search for something to eat and for the road home.

And then she saw it! The tracks made by a wagon and team of horses in the new snow. She could tell that it was a fresh trail. Then she saw wisps of straw scattered around and heard the loud barking of dogs. She eagerly followed an old snake fence that she saw there.

The fence led her to a little lean-to shed and a sagging cabin. Barking dogs came snarling at her, and in a moment she knew where she was. It was the home of the man her brothers called the Old Hermit. They had often talked about the queer old man and his strange ways. Rumor had it that he was a very shady character.

Pearly hesitated a moment at the gate held in place by binder twine. Then the dogs made up her mind for her. They rushed toward her, snarling and snapping, and Pearly turned and ran.

Later that day she found a bush—a straggly, leafless bush, but on one of its bare branches hung two red, somewhat wizened berries. A dish of strawberries and cream would have been no more tempting to the starving child. She ate them hungrily and relished the thought of her meal for several minutes. Then suddenly she became violently sick.

As the day came to a close, Pearly once more had to find a shelter from the wind and probable snow. She began to think of home. And her brothers and sisters. There were times when she had quarreled with her sisters and had become cross at her brothers' teasing. And she had grumbled about the porridge at times. How different she would be when she got back again!

She wondered what her family was doing that night. She hoped they weren't too anxious about her. Eventually, she found a place where she could rest, so she curled up, pulled her calico dress well down over her legs, and tried to keep warm. If she should never get home, she thought suddenly; if she should die out here on the prairie, the almost-new dress she had on would be wasted. How glad one of her sisters would be to have it. A tear trickled down her cheek, but in exhaustion she slept.

The fourth day dawned crisp and cold. A heavy white frost lay on the ground and a thin sheet of ice covered the little depressions where the snow of the previous night had fallen and then melted. Once more Pearly had to wait until the sun was high in the sky before her body could coax enough warmth from the rays to venture forth.

Then she walked, trusted, and searched.

Forty Royal Canadian Mounted Police were also searching. So were the people of the whole district. The doctor told the family they might as well give up, for the child couldn't possibly survive in such weather. She couldn't stand the exposure and the hunger. If she were found alive, she would be a raving lunatic.

On the fifth day the neighbors abandoned the search.

But Pearly was very much alive and fully confident that somehow her prayers would be answered. In the afternoon she found herself in a densely wooded area. The thick branches of the evergreens shut out most of the sun's rays, and it seemed almost twilight.

Suddenly there was a cracking of dried twigs just ahead. She stopped in her tracks, straining to listen and peer into the brush. She saw two big greenish eyes looking at her. The eyes belonged to a large gray timber wolf.

For a moment panic seized her. Behind the wolf came his mate. Every hair on their backs bristled as they sniffed the air, coming closer and closer. Pearly sent up a quick prayer and looked straight at the bulky gray creatures. On they came, within fifteen feet. Then they stopped and looked inquiringly at the queer human enemy.

As quickly as they had come, they circled around her and went off into the woods.

Later that day Pearly could feel the earth trembling. A pounding sound came to her ears, and a cloud of dust rose and swelled ahead. She made out the forms of horses, a thundering herd of wild horses. She was right in the path of the snorting, pawing animals.

Almost miraculously she spied tall grass nearby. She ran into it, crouching low as the stampede thundered by.

The ground there felt marshy. She dug in the soft muddy ground until a little murky water oozed up. She laid grass across the little depression and tried to sip the water, omitting the bugs, but once more she became violently ill.

It all seemed so futile, searching for a little nine-year-old girl in a calico dress with no sweater and barefoot in freezing weather. For six days and nights she had been exposed. The neighbors all gave up and began rounding up the horses for the late fall plowing that had been postponed for the search. Only the Hallberg family kept hope that she would be found.

Time dragged for the little girl, but she walked on and on. She hardly felt the hunger pangs anymore, but her feet and hands hurt terribly. At night the mournful cry of the coyote lulled her to sleep. The sixth morning she arose and prayed that that day something would happen.

When the seventh morning came, her strength was gone. She crawled painfully onto a little knoll and sat there hoping that the sun would shine very brightly, for her very bones felt chilled. It seemed ages since she had waved a happy goodbye to her mother, who had stood anxiously watching her skip down the road.

Suddenly, a boy on horseback reined up near her. She was startled, but then she recognized him as one of the nearest neighbors. He was too astonished to speak. His jaw dropped, and he just stared.

"Will you please take me home? I'm lost." Pearly said as she stumbled over to the speechless boy.

The youth jumped from his horse. He picked Pearly up tenderly and placed her on the horse and then swung up behind her, holding her carefully.

Pearly had been able to ride any horse almost as well as any man could, but this time the jolting was more than she could bear. It seemed every bone in her body was loose and hitting against her stomach. At last she cried, "Please let me down, oh, please! Please leave me here and go tell my mother."

The boy reluctantly reined his horse to a stop and then put the child down gently. She seemed so calm it surprised him. He was certain her mind had been affected. The doctor had told them all over and over that the child's nervous system would be so impaired her mind would be definitely unbalanced. But she talked very rationally and promised to wait right where they had stopped until he returned.

The boy spurred his horse all the way home and then hitched the horse to a wagon in which he and his mother and sisters hurriedly made a soft bed of feather pillows and blankets. Then he was off to get Pearly.

The Hallbergs were overcome when they opened the door and heard the news: The lost girl is found! They couldn't bring themselves to ask the question uppermost in their minds: "Is she still alive?"

The neighbor, not given to much conversation, only stated that his son had found the child.

Mother and Father Hallberg silently hitched up the team, placed in the wagon box a sheet in which to wrap the body, and started on their way. The trip was made in silence. Their hearts were too full to speak.

When Pearly was carried into the neighbor's home, her eyes lighted with joy as she saw the dinner table set with a feast to delight a queen. The tantalizing smells were too much for her. Great sobs shook her body, and she became violently ill again. So she had to be satisfied at the moment with a few sips of very weak herb tea. Just wait till my mother comes, she thought to herself. Just wait!

At last Mother and Father Hallberg stood in the doorway. Pearly lifted her hand weakly and cried, "Mother."

Mrs. Hallberg had the girl in her arms in an instant. Tears flowed freely for a while. The father stood nearby saying over and over, "Thank God. Thank God." At last the sobbing child and overjoyed mother dried their tears and smiled at each other.

The sheet in the wagon was replaced by borrowed pillows and patchwork quilts. Never had a bed felt better to Pearly's tired, aching bones. What rejoicing in the little prairie home there was that night.

Little by little Pearly regained her strength. People from miles around began to flock to hear the story of her strange adventure. They shook their heads and wondered how it had all happened. Pearly only smiled and told them of her trust in her heavenly Father. "He cared for me," she said. ❧

*A*s I read this story, my mind led me back to my last hospitalization when only a medical miracle kept me alive. During those interminable days and nights when I was kept alive by machines, I was mesmerized by watching the blips on the dials, the undulations. I couldn't help thinking: What if the roller-coaster ups and downs just stop? That would bring closure to all my dreams.

At such moments, one realizes that God and constant communication with Him are our only constants. Nothing else matters.

Ask in Faith, Nothing Wavering

Adelma Gladys Bates

"Welcome" was the simple message read by friend or stranger when he climbed the stone steps that led to the trim cottage in Evans Lane. Everyone who knew those who lived within was aware that it wasn't just an empty word used to grace the doormat, for many a tired, hungry wayfarer had found the hospitality of this friendly home awaiting them.

It was the bright smile of Myra Davis that most adorned the place. But mere adornment was not its intent, for she found real joy in sharing her happiness with others. Perhaps the constant care her mother required in her illness had intensified her willingness to brighten life's drabness in ways that only Myra could.

She it was who washed and starched the fluffy yellow curtains at the kitchen windows and baked the flaky apple pies that filled the house with their aroma, which drifted down the lane each Friday morning. She too had trimmed the shrubbery that lined the walk and trained the scarlet rambler to bend its beauty over the porch near Mother's window.

Poor Mother, Myra thought, and she sighed as she bent to cut the grass choking the pansies. Her mother's heart condition had been critically worse of late, but she was extremely patient when her bad spells came. If only she didn't suffer so! Myra prayed constantly that the Lord would spare Mother pain and not take her suddenly when Myra wasn't near to bring the relief that Dr. Thomas had provided. With good care Mother would live for years, he had told them; it was only these sudden attacks that were dangerous.

She glanced through the open window to where Mother lay, her ashen face turned toward the light. Her lips were moving. "Myra," she was whispering, "hurry!"

Dropping the grass shears, Myra ran quickly up the steps, through the kitchen, and into the adjoining room. Despite the fact that her mother's calls had been frequent of late, she felt alarmed as she saw how unusually pale she looked now.

Without hesitation Myra began the routine to which she had become accustomed. She wheeled the oxygen tank from the closet to the bedside, and she carefully adjusted the valve after hurriedly placing the tent over the pale, gasping patient.

In a few moments she sighed in relief, for her mother's white face had flushed slightly and she was breathing normally. Within an hour Mother had fallen asleep. The tent was removed and the tank returned to the closet.

It was sundown. Myra sat by the open window watching the twilight steal across the valley and listening to the woodland concert in the nearby grove of evergreens. A nightingale's lusty notes all but drowned out the call of a whippoorwill and a brown thrush. From the distance a great horned owl called gloomily. When the moon rose behind the hill she was still sitting there, watching its silvery beams until they found the brook below the house.

Myra's reverie was broken by a sudden choking sound. Turning, she switched on the light. Mother was breathing with difficulty again. Quickly, Myra prepared to administer the oxygen again. Turning the handle, she waited for the familiar sound. The silence was ominous. *There was no more oxygen!*

Myra was terrified. What could she do? The tank had scarcely been used since it had been delivered. Surely it couldn't have been emptied already.

She tried again. Could it be possible that by mistake the hospital had sent out a tank that was almost empty? The sufferer's eyes sought hers.

"Just a minute, Mother," Myra said quietly and then she turned and fled from the bedside.

"O heavenly Father," Myra prayed from the corner of her room, "please help me to know what to do. Send help, Lord, for I cannot leave Mother while she is this way."

Myra could not but marvel at the calm that came to her while she prayed. Quickly she returned to the gasping woman. Even if she were to call the doctor or the hospital, she feared help would arrive too late.

"Mother," she began, scarcely knowing just what she would say, and surprising herself when she finished the sentence, "you must try to manage without the oxygen for a few minutes. Try to breathe as normally as you can for a while to see if you can strengthen your respiratory system. Will you try?"

Her mother's eyes closed and she attempted to nod in reply.

At that moment there was a knock on the door. When Myra opened it, she found their nearest neighbor, Mrs. Parker, standing there.

She was attempting to apologize for her late call when the girl all but swept her off her feet in welcome.

"Oh, Mrs. Parker, I'm *so* glad you came. I've been praying that someone would! Surely you are the answer to that prayer," and she dabbed at the corner of her eye with the hem of her apron while she told the older woman what had happened.

Mrs. Parker suggested she call the police emergency squad at once, because the hospital ambulance was usually out on call. The telephone operator supplied the number, and the police promised to send immediate aid.

Myra returned to her mother's room and knelt by the bed. The gasps were coming more quickly now. The suffering eyes looked imploringly into her own.

"Now," the woman choked, looking at the gauge.

Calmly, Myra placed the tent in its proper position and turned on the valve. There was no sound.

"Father, all things are in Thy hands," she prayed silently as she bowed by her mother's side.

Suddenly a radiant glow seemed to fill the room. Was there a heavenly hand upon her shoulder? A voice whispered, "When thou passest through the waters, I will be with thee; and through the rivers, they shall not overflow thee."

The girl was trembling. Surely she was in the very presence of a divine being. She had done all that she could; now heaven had sent aid that no human being could give. All fear vanished, and she raised her head in grateful adoration.

The light was gone, but her mother lay resting quietly. *The oxygen was flowing freely into the tent!*

It was nearly half an hour later when the new supply of oxygen was brought from the local hospital and replaced the empty tank that had so miraculously provided life for Mrs. Davis.

Myra stood at the window watching Mrs. Parker disappear down the moonlit lane until she was lost in the shadows of the night.

"Surely," she said softly, "God *does* work in mysterious ways His wonders to perform!" ❧

*O*ne day when I was working for Boulder Memorial Hospital, I noticed a table graced by a half-dozen of the most beautiful women I had ever seen. I later asked who they were. The answer: "Oh, they're young women who are suffering from anorexia and bulimia. No matter how little or how much food they eat—it's never enough!"

It's hard enough for those suffering from these maladies, but what about their parents, their siblings—what about them?

One More Prayer for Jenny

Jewell Johnson

Alone in the darkness, with tears blinding my eyes as I tried to follow the beam of the headlights on the highway, I came to a decision. "I can't pray another prayer for Jenny," I declared.

I was sick of the eating disorder that tormented our oldest daughter. The smell of vomit in our bathroom. The arguments my husband and I had about where to hide the food so Jenny wouldn't devour it on her night binges. I was tired of our younger children complaining, "Mom, my candy is all gone. Who took it?" "Where's the sandwich meat for my lunch? It's not in the refrigerator."

I resented the tension our family experienced at mealtimes as we watched Jenny empty every bit of food onto her plate and stuff it into her mouth. Then she'd rush to the bathroom to purge herself. I wanted to divorce myself from the ugliness of bulimia and the devastation it had created as it raged through our home.

Why should I keep praying for Jenny? Hadn't I called her name in prayer every day for thirteen years and yet nothing changed?

If I quit praying, the pain of seeing our beautiful daughter teetering on the edge of ruin might stop. If I ceased hoping for a miracle, I wouldn't be disappointed again and again. Perhaps if I stopped begging God to heal Jenny, the dark cloud of depression I lived under would miraculously lift. After that dark night I prayed for other people but I never mentioned Jenny's name.

A month later I made a similar decision. This time it was about a houseplant. A geranium plant stood by the window in the bedroom, the best spot in our house for growing things. I had watered it with rainwater and fertilized it, yet it refused to flourish. Now it was one green stalk with a few sickly yellow leaves struggling to stay alive. It had been that way for months.

"You're not going to grow?" I asked the plant that day. "OK, I'm done pampering you! Out you go!" I picked up the heavy pot and stomped through the house to the garage.

As I tipped the pot, ready to dump the plant into the garbage can, a voice challenged me. *So, you're going to throw it out just like you did Jenny?*

Jenny? I questioned. *What . . . what do you mean?*

The voice continued. *You threw Jenny out of your prayers. Don't you know the sickest need more time and patience and the hopeless need more care and prayer?*

Had I heard right? Though the words weren't audible, I heard them in my heart, and the message was clear. I had abandoned my daughter at her lowest point, when she needed my prayers and support the most.

I sank to the garage steps. Salty tears dripped into the black dirt as I sobbed, "God, I love her so much. I want her to be a whole person. Why, God, didn't You answer my prayers?"

Wiping my eyes, I hoisted the plant into my arms and headed back into the house. At that moment something happened: I determined—I *vowed*—to again pray for Jenny. How long? One month, two months, a year? Now the time didn't matter. My faith was renewed, and I'd pray for her as long as I had breath.

Jenny's recovery came slowly. She suffered from weakness and hair loss. A dentist told her the enamel on her front teeth had become dangerously thin from years of purging.

"If I lose my teeth, I don't want to live!" she declared. I braced for the worst.

This time Jenny turned to Scripture. "Mom," she said, "the Bible says God will restore what the locust and cankerworm have devoured. Can I ask God to heal my teeth when I'm the one who ruined them?"

"Healing is a gift," I said. "Yes, you can ask God to heal your teeth." Soon afterwards the dentist began treatments to preserve the thinned enamel.

Every day was a struggle as Jenny tried to relearn normal eating patterns. Often, she'd slip back into the old habit of gorging and purging. I stood by, cheering her better days and praying on good days and bad.

With encouragement, tears, and prayers, Jenny worked toward physical, mental, and emotional healing. One day she said, "Things are shaky, Mom, but God and I together—we're going to make it. Just keep praying!"

What happened to the geranium plant? It stands in our living room—growing, flourishing, and reminding me every day that with God, there are no hopeless cases. There are no limits to what He can do as we keep on praying. ❧

The life of a missionary is often romanticized by those who have never experienced it. Many the heroic men and women who have suffered an early death in tropic climes. This particular story took place many years ago.

SAVED BY A SONG

As told to Robert Strickland

Since daylight, I had been trudging along a winding trail, and now at midday the sun was pouring down upon me with a power that was almost prostrating. Summertime in Central America is always a trying season for foreigners who have not been long away from the mild, invigorating atmosphere of more northern climes. That day I realized that the intense heat and strain of my means of travel had sapped my store of physical strength to almost the limit of endurance.

My purpose in making this journey was to find an isolated Spanish Christian who was reported to be living about forty miles north of the city of Port Limon. Having set out in the very early morning, I had hoped to reach his house by noon. However, my plans had greatly miscarried. It had been according to expectation that I should walk much of the way; but my plans did not call for the entire journey on foot and the necessity of pushing a heavily laden bicycle that bore a fairly complete supply of books in addition to my wearing apparel and other personal belongings.

The faint trail led through marsh and jungle and over stony hillocks and almost impenetrable bush land. Millions of mosquitoes thrived everywhere. My face, neck, and wrists were soon practically raw from their continual attacks. Perspiration trickled into my eyes, dropped from my chin, fell off my hands, ran down my back in little streams, and squished in my shoes when I stepped. I was soaking wet, thirsty, and feeling famished, yet there was not a drop of water to drink. My throat felt as if it had been scalded; my face burned, every joint in my body ached, and weakness seized me, but still I struggled on.

For hours, no sign of a house or hut had been seen. The odometer on my bicycle showed that I had come slightly more than seventeen miles. Where was I? I didn't know except that this threatening wilderness surrounded me on all sides. Malaria was taking a firm grip on me. It would be impossible for me to reach my destination that day, for I knew I couldn't go much farther, nor would I have been able to retrace my steps to town had I known the way. Lost! And in such a place as this!

The path now skirted the foot of a steep hill, running along the edge of a jungle marsh. Alligators were sunning themselves and lolling at ease in the greenish shallow waters. I couldn't move the bicycle an inch farther. I stopped to lean upon it, and a dizzy nausea possessed me. What must I do? To remain in the jungle at night would mean almost certain death. Discouraging thoughts pressed in, sorely besetting my feeble mind and affecting even my strength of body.

But I knew that there was in my possession the key to the storehouse of our heavenly Father's strength, and to Him I turned. From my heart I cried: "Dear Lord, forgive. Never could I doubt Thy boundless love and mercy, only teach me to trust and see the purpose of Thy will. And now have pity on Thy servant. I am weak and faint and weary, lost and helpless. My Father, I pray that Thou reach down Thy great strong arm in love and help me."

"Anywhere with Jesus I can safely go.
Anywhere He leads in this world below;
Anywhere without Him, dearest joys
    would fade.
Anywhere with Jesus I am not afraid."

Music, soft, clear, and appealing! Floating gently, down to me it came, the voice of a child singing. Was this a dream, or could it be the seductive influence of delirium? This was a land where the English language was not spoken, and many hours had passed since last I had seen human habitation. Perhaps my faith wasn't ready to recognize the immediate answer to prayer. I stood as if bound with wonder as the unseen singer continued:

"Anywhere with Jesus I am not alone.
Other friends may fail me. He is still my
    own.
Though His hand may lead me over dreary
    ways.
Anywhere with Jesus is a house of praise."

Here, summoning all my reserve strength, I shouted, "Who is singing?"

The bushes on the hillside were moving. In a few seconds some tropical shrubs were drawn apart, and a little face appeared brightened by two shining eyes that stared at me in wonder and startled pleasure.

"Child, was that you singing?" I asked the little girl.

"Yes, sir," she replied in very good English.

"Where did you learn that song?" I questioned.

Her reply came quickly: "At Sabbath school."

"Sabbath school!" I exclaimed in surprise. "Is there a Sabbath school around here anywhere?"

"No, sir, I learned it at Sabbath school in Barbados."

"Barbados!" That was another surprise, for Barbados was more than a thousand miles away. I asked another question: "What are you doing here?"

"Why, we live here now, up there on the top of the hill," she said, pointing.

"Is there a way for me to get up to your house?" I asked.

With a nimble spring she landed in the path where I stood and started down it in the direction from which I had just come, beckoning to me to follow, as she said, "Yes, sir, come this way. I'll show you."

Going only a few feet, the child pulled aside a heavy growth of vines, disclosing a well-worn footpath ascending the hillside. "So you went to Sabbath school in Barbados," I remarked as I turned into the opening she had made.

"Yes, sir, but we don't have regular Sabbath school here. There are none who keep the Sabbath but ourselves."

The climb, together with the weight of the bicycle, was too much for me, and I dropped upon the root of a nearby tree, permitting the "wheel" to roll on till it chose to stop in a heap on the ground at no great distance.

Then, gaining my breath, I sought to resume the conversation by saying, "How many are in your family?"

"Just me and my mamaw and my papaw, but we want to have a meeting tonight anyway. You will preach for us, won't you, Elder?" said she, bringing another surprise to me.

"What makes you think I am an elder?" I asked.

"Oh," she said, "I know who you are. You are Elder _____. I have your picture."

Another surprise. "Where did you get my picture?"

"It is on the Kingston church calendar that papaw got from a man he met when he was in Colon," came the reply.

"What is your name?" I asked.

"Ellen Young," she answered between puffs, as she tussled with my bicycle in a successful effort to get it up the hill.

Watching the little girl struggle with the heavy burden of the bicycle stirred me, and I climbed on up the hill too, though my weakened condition would permit me to do but little at a time, and I was obliged to stop often for rest ere the top was reached.

Arriving at the house (a two-room thatched hut), Ellen darted in and placed a chair for me, then dashed out with all speed to return in but a moment with two green coconuts from which the ends had been severed with a sharp machete. The sight was a welcome one indeed, and as I drank the cool, sweet coconut water so thoughtfully provided, I silently offered to God my thanksgiving for His having heard the cry of His needy servant.

Refreshed, I learned that the family had come from Barbados only recently, and that they had been living in this place but three months. The child's father and mother were working on a nearby banana plantation and would have been summoned had I not protested. I did not wish them to leave their labor before it was time for them to stop and thus incur the displeasure of their employer.

Ellen brought out a package of carefully treasured Sabbath school papers that had been given her in Barbados; she showed me a *Gospel Primer* that was hers; and she pointed to a copy of *Christ in Song* as one of her treasures. After this display of her wealth, my little hostess inquired if I had had any dinner, and on learning that I had eaten only a few water biscuits (a plain, hard cracker much used in the tropics), she went out again, but returned presently with a nice, big, ripe, juicy papaw [papaya]. Her intelligence and thoughtfulness impressed me as being a forceful testimony to the power of the gospel in developing minds and forming character.

"Do you know," I said to her, "I don't like to think what might have happened to me if you hadn't gone to the hillside and sung that song. I was sick and tired, and but for the fact that the Lord sent you to find me, I would, no doubt, be lost somewhere in the jungle now."

"Miss Nina—that was my teacher in Barbados," she explained—"told us we ought to sing every day. She said singing would keep us from having bad or worthless thoughts, and she said it is possible that a child's singing would sometimes bring people to Jesus."

"Your teacher taught you right, my child," I assured her. "Jesus wants His children to be happy and to sing His praises. Your singing has today been a great help to me, and by continuing, you may, as your Miss Nina has said, lead someone to Christ."

For a child of her age, Ellen was surprisingly familiar with the Scriptures. One of the greatest longings of her little life was to own a Bible all her very own. In the parcel carrier on my bicycle, where I always carried Bibles and books when out on trips of this kind, there was a new British and Foreign Bible Society Bible of a suitable size for such a child. It was bound in morocco. Taking this book out, I wrote on the flyleaf: "To my dear little friend. Ellen Young, / In appreciation of the great good that came to me from her singing 'Anywhere With Jesus.' / May this blessed book be your constant companion and daily guide. / Elder _____. (Date)"

In the more than thirty years of my connection with the gospel ministry, it has been my pleasure to distribute many Bibles, but never have I known one to be received with such joy, gladness, and demonstration of thankfulness as were shown by that little girl when I placed the Book of books in her hands. A brief moment she stared at me in surprise, eyes and mouth wide open, perhaps thinking her ears had deceived her; but when she finally realized that the beautiful new Bible was *really* hers, a look of supreme happiness spread over her face, and in joy she cried: "Thank you, thank you, thank you, Elder! Oh, I am so glad! I didn't know it was going to be really mine."

"I'm glad you like it, Ellen."

"I like it better than *anything*, better than *all the things I have ever had in all my life!* Now I can let Jesus talk to me, can't I?"

"Indeed you can," I replied, and started to say more, but the eager little face lighted up, and looking out the door, I saw a man coming along the path. He had a small bunch of green bananas on his shoulder and a machete under his arm. Toward this person the child raced, and I watched the meeting, for it was Ellen's father. The distance was too great for me to hear the words, but I saw her displaying her new treasure. The man seized her hand and started toward the house in such haste that soon they were both running.

When he came within hearing distance, I heard him saying, "Thank the Lord, thank the Lord." When he spied me, he shouted gleefully. "Elder, howdy! Thank the Lord He did send a preacher. Elder, I'm sure glad to see you. Ain't the Master real good to His poor children? I found some poor folks that want to know about Him, and I tell them all I can. Then when I can't do any more, I ask the Lord to send us a minister, and here you come. The good Lord shure do answer prayer. Ain't that grand?"

"Yes," I answered, "the Lord certainly does answer our prayers." But I was thinking of my own recent experience, and marveling that I felt so much better. It seemed that the fever was leaving me almost entirely.

It was not long after the father's arrival till the barking of the family dog announced the mother's return. Ellen also ran to meet her, proudly showing her Bible and heralding the minister's presence in their home. At the announcement, the mother, daughter, and even the dog ran for joy to meet this man whom God had sent. On the way, the woman's emotional nature expressed itself as she exclaimed: "Thank Jesus, our prayers is answered. Praise the Lord for His blessings to us. I knowed the Lord was going to bless me, I been feeling it all day. How you do, Elder?" This last as she came into the house. "How did you find us? The Lord sure did send you here." Then wistfully, "You goin' to have a meetin' tonight, ain't we, Elder?"

Without waiting for me to reply, the host

spoke: "Yes, we are going to have a meeting tonight. That's what the Lord sent the elder here for. You fix supper. I'm going over to tell the folks about the meetin', and see if we can't get the Taylors to come."

Just before dark he returned and happily reported that two families had promised to attend the meeting. A good, substantial supper of white yams, rice, and boiled green bananas was served, and before the table was cleared, the visitors began to arrive, from where, in what I had thought to be wild jungle, I know not. The company, besides the Young family, consisted of three men, two women, and two girls a little older than Ellen.

The subject of the discourse was the second coming of Christ. No audience within my knowledge ever received the message more gladly. They were loath to leave, and insisted on hearing more, so I felt forced to give a Bible study on the various phases of the Christian life. This occupied much time, finally drifting into a talk on the love of God. Many times during the studies that evening little Ellen found the texts that were announced and read the passages. The visitors were amazed at her ability, because never before had they seen even a grown person, much less a child, who could turn readily to any scripture cited.

Eleven o'clock came, and the hearers were not tired, and it had not once crossed their minds that the man whom God had sent to instruct them might be weary. "Parson," said a man named Macey, "tell us about heaven and hell. Do good people go to heaven when they die, and the no-count ones go to hell? I don't understand them things at all."

In response to this request, we took up quite a complete study of the nature of man and were gratified to find by nods and expressions of assent, that the seed was falling in good soil. At the close of that study, Macey said: "That explains it. Now I understand lots of things that were puzzles before."

"Just think, Brudder Macey," said Taylor, "here we's been all these years and didn't know all them good things was in God's Book. Brudder Young, I do shure thank the Lord you brought me here tonight to hear this gospel."

Still they wanted to know about the home of the saved, so I preached again, stressing the point that only God's real commandment-keeping children will inherit the land to share the glories of God, while those who walked with the world will be destroyed in the final conflagration when the earth shall melt with heat, and all the works therein be burned up.

It was well into the morning when I finished preaching. The two visiting children had fallen asleep hours before, but Ellen had bravely remained awake, seeming to drink in every word that was spoken, until about two o'clock, when she fell asleep with her Bible open in her lap. On finishing the last sermon, an appeal was made to those present to decide the great question as to whether they would walk with God's commandment keepers or not.

The man Macey was upon his feet instantly. "I have decided," he said. "God has set the pearly gates ajar tonight, and I have seen the blazing glory from within. I'm done with sin and done with the old devil. It's me and Jesus now and forever." Turning to his wife, he said earnestly, "What you goin' to do about it, honey? Don't this blessed truth look sweet to you?"

"Yes, Tom," she answered. "Praise the Lord for His goodness! How I do thank Him for what I have learned tonight!"

Tears of happiness flowed. Taylor and his companion and Taylor's wife wanted to decide the question then and there also, but they were under a contract with their employer and felt that they should talk it over with him before they began to keep the Sabbath.

Next day, Ellen undertook to wash my perspiration-soaked clothes, and when they were dry, she smoothed them with an iron heated in an open fire built in the yard. She did a fine job, too, for such a little girl. After this work was finished, I taught her how to use the references and marginal readings in her Bible, and in the late afternoon she piloted me to visit a sick woman, whose misery was made lighter by the girl's ministry.

That night there was quite a gathering for the meeting, more than the house would hold, so I preached in the yard, where several torches were kept burning to supply light. It was hard to leave those interested and heart-hungry people, but as I set out early the next morning, my host and Ellen accompanied me for the first three miles. Finally we came to the place in the road where they must turn back.

Taking the man's hand, I wished him heaven's rich blessing and thanked him for kindly coming so far on the way with me. Then turning to Ellen, I placed my hands on her head and prayed God to bless the little life that had brought help to me and joy to others. As we knelt, we united our petitions to God in behalf of those in that place who were starting to walk with Him.

A little way down the path I stopped and looked back. There was Ellen, holding her Bible and clinging to her father's hand. He shouted, "Goodbye, Elder. If we don't meet down here again, let's meet on the sea of glass." I waved, and in another moment a turn in the road lost them to sight.

Many years have passed since then, but even now, sometimes when I am weary and the way is hard, it seems to me I can hear echoes of that sweet voice singing,

Anywhere with Jesus I can safely go.
Anywhere He leads me in this world
    below. ❦

*I*f you examine a map of the world, you will eventually find a tiny dot—one of the most remote places in the world—in the vast Pacific Ocean. The island gained its fame from the Mutiny on the Bounty *film and the Bounty trilogy by Nordhoff and Hall* (Mutiny on the Bounty, Men Against the Sea, *and* Pitcairn's Island*). I have long been fascinated by the island and, when younger, collected its stamps. (Pitcairn is a British protectorate.) Thus, when I came across this story, I read it, archived a copy, and left it there to gestate. Perhaps the day might come when it would be needed to complete a story anthology.*

Its time has come!

PROVIDENCE ON PITCAIRN

Roy P. Clark

It was a beautiful, starlit morning when we pushed off from the island in two of our boats to meet the steamer due to arrive shortly after dawn. The sea was calm and peaceful, and there was every indication that the coming day would be a real tropical one. Off Bounty Bay a few hundred yards a small yacht lay idly at anchor. We came alongside the craft, and one of our boat's crew called out, "Ship ahoy, *Karlchris.*" There was no response, and someone muttered, "Guess they're all in their bunks yet."

But a minute or two later a tousled head appeared above the hatch, and we heard Bill, the captain of the cruiser, say, "You boys are up pretty early. What's the idea?" Our coxswain called out, "Hello, Bill, you goin' off to meet the steamer with us?" Yes, Bill was. He disappeared below deck, and in a short time made himself ready, jumped into our boat, and we cast off.

The sun had not yet risen, but the gray, low-lying clouds in the east showed that old King Sol was not far below the horizon. We made ourselves as comfortable as possible while we awaited the arrival of the steamer, expected to be off Bounty Bay at six o'clock. Behind us, as the light increased, the contour of the island began to shape itself into hills and valleys. Trees and shrubbery separated from the darkness and became distinct from each other. Houses appeared amid the foliage, and our island began to reveal its rugged beauty in the early light.

The sun in front of us was about to rise. What a glorious sight to watch the clouds gradually "catch fire" as the red glow became more intense. With the sudden appearance of the sun, the island was bathed in rays of golden light. A new day had been ushered in by the omnipotence of God—the beginning of a perfect day, we thought then. But before sundown we would experience a day of anguish such as few of the islanders had seen in all their lives.

Someone called out, "Sail-o-o-o-o," and

we all looked to the west beyond Matt's Rock. There we sighted the American tanker for which we had been waiting. All hands in both boats came to life, and in no time we were pulling out to sea to meet the oncoming steamer.

An hour later, after we had exchanged our island produce for what merchandise we needed, we pulled away from the vessel and headed toward land. As we pulled away, we noticed with some misgivings that the swells were increasing in size and that the seas at the landing place were much stronger than they had been when we left a few hours ago. However, this fact hardly caused comment, for often the sea and surf change quickly around the island. We came alongside the *Karlchris* and Bill jumped aboard. We cast off once more, headed for the passage, and made the harbor without difficulty.

Two hours later there was some excitement among the school children. Someone called out, "Look at the surf!" The boys and girls rushed to the cliff near the school to watch the great swells rolling in. The waves broke with a roaring hiss and sent the spray high into the air. It was a beautiful sight, but also a fearful one.

In the afternoon we heard the long, drawn-out call of Sail-O for the second time that day. Someone had sighted a steamer heading directly for the island, so a dispatch of mail was quickly made up by the postmaster and carried to the landing, where most of the islanders had gathered. "Could the boats get out through the passage?" they asked. "Is it safe to attempt it?"

Finally, some of the men decided they would try to take the boats through. In pairs and singly the men solemnly went down the steep narrow path to the beach. Only one boat was hauled into the harbor, for the tide was high and strong even inside the sheltered cove. The longboat had to be held close to the beach until the crew jumped in and took their places at their oars. They made the open sea safely and reached the visiting vessel without difficulty.

When the steamer blew its departing whistle at about dusk, the crew scrambled back into their boat and pulled quickly for shore in order to make the harbor before darkness set in. By this time the waves were huge. Continual rows of heavy combers pounded the shore and raced in through the passage. For some time the oncoming seas hindered the boat from being pulled through the narrow opening in the rocks.

The delay was fatal. It appeared that there never would be a time when the sea was sufficiently quiet to permit the boat to pass into the harbor. At last one of the crew shouted out, "Pull ahead!" The boat darted forward as if sensing its danger, but a large wave rose just behind it, doubled over, and completely enveloped both the boat and the crew. The next swell capsized the boat, and the crew were thrown into the churning waters of the passage or trapped beneath the overturned boat.

The onlookers ashore stood aghast, panic stricken. They were mostly women and children, for nearly all the island men had gone toward the ship. Darkness had now settled in, and the upturned boat could not be seen. Those who knew the sea were certain that it had drifted out to sea rather than instead of being washed ashore. Women started to weep and wail for loved ones whom they thought were drowned. For how could a man live in such a turbulent sea? It seemed impossible. Some of the women were so overcome with grief that they could not move, and sat like statues on the beach, frozen with fear. Pitiful cries ascended to God for the protection of the men.

A few of the women and older children began to search along the rocks for the battered men, some of whom might have been washed ashore dead or alive. Four were found. Two were injured, and two were unhurt.

The handful of men ashore sprang into action and attempted the impossible, or so it seemed to all of us. The captain of one of the longboats shouted, "Haul down the barge." Almost instantly a second boat was in the harbor. "I want volunteers who will go out there to save those men."

Eight islanders responded. Most of them are fearless sailors in the roughest weather, and here was a sea to test their mettle. The waves thundered in through the passage with a crash and roar. The harbor itself seemed alive with fury. Two men held the boat so that it too would not be swept ashore by the inrush of current through the narrow opening.

Women and children begged their husbands and fathers not to go out. But above the babble of voices and the boisterous sound of the surf the captain called out, "Where's Cook? Where's Cook? Get up to the White Rocks!" Cook was not to be found. We learned later he had been some distance along the shore searching for bodies. One of the men holding the boat left for the White Rocks to signal the men below when it seemed the most suitable time to send the boat out from the beach.

The men in the boat waited, some fearful yet anxious to make an effort to save their fellow men. Finally the call came from the lookout, "Pull ahead." That night, while the boat was leaving the beach for the passage, the islanders prayed as they had never prayed before, for everyone thought there was only one chance in a thousand that they would make it to the open sea. But the miracle happened. The impossible was done. The crew and boat sped through the little opening in the rocks as if guided by unseen hands. Let us not attribute all this to chance. It would be blasphemous.

Seaward was Cimmerian darkness. Those ashore waited—some eager and expectant; and some with utter hopelessness—for news to be flashed by torchlight. Moments seemed ages. Sobbing could be heard here and there along the beach. Others in groups talked in low tones. The suspense was unbearable.

The two wounded men stayed on the beach, where they were made comfortable, and would not let anyone carry them home until they heard the news. One or two men were up at the White Rocks waiting for flash signals. Time passed. It seemed to be interminable, but in reality it was only half an hour when the call came: "All is well!"

No sweeter or more welcome words were ever heard by Pitcairn islanders. The thing that could not happen *did* happen. Was it true? Many could not believe it. It seemed impossible. From ashore the signal was flashed, "Is it true?" The return answer buoyed up doubtful hearts, "All is well, Nelson speaking."

Later we were told how the rescue boat had found the lost men. As soon as they were safely free from the surf and outside the harbor, they began their search. Rays of torchlight pierced the darkness in every direction. Of course, the men clinging to the boat shouted for help, but the roar of the sea drowned their voices. The current was setting off strongly to the east, so the search was made in that direction. Finally a beam of light brought men and boat into view. They were dangerously near the rocks, in the heavy swells, and were struggling to cling to the keel. Some had a hand-hold on the sides of the boat. Many of the men were utterly exhausted, and those who could swim the best helped those who could not. It was certain that they saved five or six from drowning.

The yacht *Karlchris* came on the scene, but had to keep a good distance from the shore. The rescue boat, with its nine men, and as many of the rescued as could pull an oar, towed the capsized boat toward the yacht. Many of the men clambered aboard, but a full crew remained at the oars to make every effort to save the other boat from drifting to sea.

Their efforts were futile. The current was too strong, and after several hours of trying to pull ashore they had to cut the boat adrift. It was a heart pang for all, for the island men love their surf boats.

It was dawn before the rest of the men left the *Karlchris,* jumped into the longboat, and made ready once more to brave the passage and reach land. The sea was still lashing viciously in the harbor opening, but undaunted by their recent experience, the men longed to reach shore, greet their loved ones, and get hot drinks and a change of clothing. For the second time in twenty-four hours they made ready to enter the water. The lookout man was at his place at the White Rocks. The signal was given, and this time the men were so eager and determined to reach shore that the boat simply glided over the water, but even so they were not quick enough. A great wave caught it and sped it like lightning onto the rocks. The men jumped into the harbor to save it from further disaster. Some were hurt, and one man had to be carried up to the village. This time the women came to the rescue, caught hold of the lines, and quickly hauled the boat up onto the sliding.

Never was there such a welcome between friends and loved ones, husbands and wives, as on that day when twenty-three men, most of them doomed to certain death, were miraculously spared by the mercy of God. ❧

*S*ince many of my Wheeler ancestors were sea captains, first in England and later in New England, I've always felt more than a little affinity for the sea and those most beautiful of all ships ever made: the windjammers. Perhaps because it's in my blood by inheritance and DNA, that may explain why I find it so difficult to be separated long from the sea. As for this story, my wife and I were privileged to explore the tunnels inside Gibraltar a few years ago and were fascinated by the history of that great rock fortress.

About one hundred years ago there lived in Marblehead, Massachusetts, a God-fearing sea captain named Richard Girdler, who sought to make his vessel a place of prayer, and who trusted in God amid the perils of the mighty deep.

One night he was called upon to take charge of the brig *Farnsworth,* in which he had sailed to Antwerp the preceding April, and which was now laden and ready for another long voyage.

Having arranged matters with the owners, Captain Girdler went on board the brig the next morning and found everything ready—with one exception. In his opinion, before starting on so long a voyage, the vessel needed one hawser and one kedge more than the *Farnsworth* now had.

A *hawser,* as our seafaring readers know, is strong rope used for anchoring or towing a ship. And a *kedge* is a small anchor used primarily to steady a vessel and to "warp" it where it's wanted when wind and tide are in opposition.

The captain laid the matter before the owners and received orders to procure a kedge and then go back to Marblehead to obtain there a suitable hawser for it. The kedge was easily found, but the captain couldn't get such a hawser as he wanted in all Marblehead, and there was no ropewalk there long enough to "say one" (twist one), and it was too rainy to do it out of doors. But the captain would not go without his hawser and was finally obliged to have it laid in two pieces of sixty fathoms each, which, when joined together, made a strong hawser of 120 fathoms, or 720 feet in length.

Thus provided, the *Farnsworth* cleared from the port of Boston for Liberia, on October 3, 1826, and sailed on her destined voyage. During the passage, family worship was regularly maintained, and all who could be spared from duty were invited to attend.

About the first of December, 1826, the *Farnsworth* reached the Bay of Gibraltar and came to anchor, and remained there some days, with hundreds of other vessels that were moored in the bay. On the sixth of the month the weather looked threatening—a gale seemed to be approaching. The crew made such preparations as they could for the fearful encounter; all the anchors—the small bower and the best bower and the little kedge, with the whole new hawser of one hundred twenty fathoms—were carried out, and everything was made trim and snug for a storm.

They had not long to wait. The wind freshened, and then at nine o'clock in the evening the gale burst upon them with tremendous power, and at eleven o'clock it blew a perfect hurricane. No less than three hundred vessels of all classes and descriptions had found anchorage there, and the effect of such a gale among them may be imagined. Cables parted, anchors dragged, vessels drifted hither and thither like corks upon the water, dashing against one another and upon the shore, and consternation and dismay were on every countenance.

At a quarter past eleven o'clock, the *Farnsworth* parted her small bower and began to drift with the hurricane. Soon her best bower anchor followed, and away went the brig before the wind. Up to this time, most of the vessels had gone on to the "neutral ground"; some of them little injured, some bilged, some disabled, some crushed by the collisions caused by the roll of larger vessels, and all in imminent peril, with death and destruction stalking wildly through the storm.

Just at this time the danger seemed to increase, for the wind had shifted, and the *Farnsworth* was drifting directly toward the massive breakwater against whose rocky side it seemed that it must crash beyond hope of escape. A little astern of her, a ship from New York had been dashed in pieces upon the rocks; and distinctly visible through the surrounding gloom roared the white breakers, which seemed to everyone on board to be weaving for them a winding sheet (a burial cloth).

What now could be done? No skill could avail; no human arm could save them; and He who hushed the wild waves of Gennesaret with His word, walked not upon these dark waters to quiet their tumultuous rage. Refuge failed them, and they could only prepare to meet their impending fate.

Shrinking from their awful doom, they raised their cries to God. On the very verge of destruction, the crew all kneeled upon the deck, while above the voice of deep calling unto deep arose the captain's cry to Him who is mighty to save. And he was heard. He who once slept in the hinder part of a vessel and awoke to save His disciples from the yawning waves had a care for this ship where His name was honored; and when the crew arose from their knees, they found, to their amazement, that their ship, which had been driven from her moorings when held by three anchors, was now heading toward the wind and riding securely, held only by the little kedge!

At midnight the gale abated, but the morning light disclosed a fearful scene. The "neutral ground" was packed with ill-fated vessels piled one upon another in terrible confusion. Some had gone directly upon the rocks and been dashed in pieces there; and of the three hundred vessels that were riding quietly at anchor the day before, not more than fifty remained unharmed. The rest were either wrecked or more or less injured. Four hundred seamen had perished in the gale; and the shore of Gibraltar was strewn with the fragments of wrecked vessels.

And how did the *Farnsworth* escape? She was drifting rapidly onto the rocks, and her two strongest cables and heaviest anchors were gone. How was the vessel saved from impending ruin?

The captain sent out a boat and got up his anchors; but when he came to heave up his little kedge, he found it almost impossible to raise it. Slowly and wearily they toiled to heave it up, and when it came under the vessel's bow, they saw with wonder that the fluke of the little kedge was hooked into the ring of a huge old Spanish anchor that weighed more than three thousand pounds!

God had not permitted Captain Girdler to go to sea without his little kedge. A large anchor would not answer; it must be a little kedge just large enough to steady a vessel while lying in the stream, and small enough so that the fluke of it could enter the ring of that old Spanish anchor. And it must be fastened to a new cable strong enough to hold the brig amid the fury of the gale. God knew all about it, and He knew just when to shift the wind to bring the kedge where the old anchor was and so deliver them from death by the very means that seemed to portend a more swift destruction.

Truly our Father heareth prayer. ❧

*H*aving grown up in Latin America as children of missionary parents, how well we remember those missionary shipments that churches would periodically send us. We called them "Dorcas barrels."

Rarely did we find anything in them other than hand-me-down clothes. Consequently, we'd steel ourselves for more of the same every time Dad would pry the cover off one of those containers. As for the folks, once in a while a church would send them something that they really needed—even (rarely) something new!

A Perfect Mistake

Cheryl Walterman Stewart

Grandpa Nybakken loved life—especially when he could play a trick on somebody. At those times, his large Norwegian frame would shake with laughter while he feigned innocent surprise, exclaiming, "Oh, forevermore!" But on a cold Saturday in downtown Chicago, God played a trick on him, and Grandpa wasn't laughing.

Grandpa Nybakken, mother's father, worked as a carpenter. On this particular day, he was building some crates for the clothes his church was sending to an orphanage in China. On his way home, he reached into his shirt pocket to get his glasses, but they were gone. He remembered putting them there that morning, so he drove back to the church. His search proved fruitless.

When he mentally replayed his earlier actions, he realized what had happened: the glasses had slipped out of his pocket unnoticed and fallen into one of the crates, which now were nailed shut. His brand new glasses were heading for China!

The Great Depression was at its height and Grandpa had six children. He had spent twenty dollars—a lot of money in those days—for those glasses that very morning. He was upset by the thought of having to buy another pair.

"It's not fair," he told God as he drove home in frustration. "I've been very faithful in giving of my time and money to Your work, and now this."

Several months later the director of the orphanage was on furlough in the United States. He wanted to visit all the churches that supported him in China, so one Sunday night he came to speak at my grandfather's small church in Chicago. Grandpa and his family sat in their customary seats among the sparse congregation.

The missionary began by thanking the people for their faithfulness in supporting the orphanage. "But most of all," he said, "I must thank you for the glasses you sent last year. You see, the Communists had just swept through the orphanage, destroying everything, including my glasses. I was desperate.

"Even if I had the money, there was simply no way of replacing those glasses. Along with not being able to see well, I experienced headaches every day, so my coworkers and I were much in prayer about this.

"Then your crates arrived. When my staff removed the covers, they found a pair of glasses lying on top."

The missionary paused long enough to let his words sink in. Then, still gripped with the wonder of it all, he continued: "Folks, when I tried on the glasses, it was as though they had been custom-made just for me! I want to thank you for being a part of that."

The people listened, happy for the miraculous glasses. *But the missionary surely must have confused our church with another,* they thought. *There were no glasses on our list of items to be sent overseas.*

But sitting quietly in the back, with tears streaming down his face, an ordinary carpenter realized the Master Carpenter had used him in an extraordinary way. ❦

"Introduction: The Ups and Downs of Prayer Life," by Joseph Leininger Wheeler. Copyright © 2015. Printed by permission of the author. Central to the Introduction is Philip Yancey's book *Prayer: Does It Make Any Difference?* (Grand Rapids, MI: Zondervan, 2006).

SECTION ONE
"The Wager," by Marcus Bach. Published in *The Christian Herald,* June 1963. Printed by permission of *The Christian Herald.*

"Real Courage," by Laura Nelson. Published in *The Youth's Instructor,* December 27, 1932. Reprinted by permission of Review and Herald® Publishing Association, Silver Spring, MD 20904. If anyone can provide information about the author or the author's next of kin, please send it to Joe Wheeler (P.O. Box 1246, Conifer, CO 80433).

"Soap and Bags and Hairs on My Head," by Wendy Miller. Copyright © 1997. Reprinted by permission of the author.

"A Cry for Help in the Jungle," by William Butler and W. A. Spicer. Published in Spicer's book, *The Hand That Intervenes* (Washington, DC: Review and Herald® Publishing Association, 1918). Original text owned by Joe Wheeler.

"White Walls," by Gussie Ross Jobe. Published in *The Youth's Instructor,* November 21, 1933. Reprinted by permission of Review and Herald® Publishing Association, Silver Spring, MD 20904. If anyone can provide

information about the author or the author's next of kin, please send it to Joe Wheeler (P.O. Box 1246, Conifer, CO 80433).

"If It Be God's Will," by Phyllis Jeanne Branard. Published in *The Youth's Instructor,* July 10, 1951. Reprinted by permission of Review and Herald® Publishing Association, Silver Spring, MD 20904. If anyone can provide information about the author or the author's next of kin, please send it to Joe Wheeler (P.O. Box 1246, Conifer, CO 80433).

"Angels in a Tow Truck," by Teresa A. Sales. Copyright © 2015. Printed by permission of the author.

SECTION TWO
"Alone, Yet Not Alone Am I," by Henry Melchior Muhlenberg with Regina Leininger and Maria LeRoy. Special thanks to the Leininger Family Newsletters and the archives of the State of Pennsylvania.

"How God Sent the Flour," author unknown. Published in *The Youth's Instructor,* December 18, 1923. Reprinted by permission of Review and Herald® Publishing Association, Silver Spring, MD 20904. If anyone can provide information about the author or the author's next of kin, please send it to Joe Wheeler (P.O. Box 1246, Conifer, CO 80433).

"Inches From Air," by Kent Rathbun. Published in *The Guide,* September 18, 1996. Reprinted by permission of the author.

"His Way in the Fire," by Doris Thistle. Published in *The Youth's Instructor,* April 10, 1945. Reprinted by permission of Review and Herald® Publishing Association, Silver Spring, MD 20904. If anyone can provide information about the author or the author's next of kin, please send it to Joe Wheeler (P.O. Box 1246, Conifer, CO 80433).

"A 1940 Miracle," by Phyllis Prout. Published in *The Youth's Instructor,* July 15, 1941. Reprinted by permission of Review and Herald® Publishing Association, Silver Spring, MD 20904. If anyone can provide information about the author or the author's next of kin, please send it to Joe Wheeler (P.O. Box 1246, Conifer, CO 80433).

"Four Hours Early," by Joseph Leininger Wheeler. Copyright © 2015. Printed by permission of the author.

SECTION THREE

"The Castaway of Fish Rock," by George Bond. Published in *The Youth's Instructor,* September 16, 1930. Reprinted by permission of Review and Herald® Publishing Association, Silver Spring, MD 20904. If anyone can provide information about the author or the author's next of kin, please send it to Joe Wheeler (P.O. Box 1246, Conifer, CO 80433).

"Do You Believe in Miracles?" by Rochelle Pennington. If anyone can provide information about the author's current address, please send it to Joe Wheeler (P.O. Box 1246, Conifer, CO 80433).

"The Other Boy," by Jeanette Swing. Published in *The Youth's Instructor,* April 5, 1927. Reprinted by permission of Review and Herald® Publishing Association, Silver Spring, MD 20904. If anyone can provide information about the author or the author's next of kin, please send it to Joe Wheeler (P.O. Box 1246, Conifer, CO 80433).

"The Jungle Bandmaster," by Eric B. Hare. Published in *The Youth's Instructor,* June 12, 1928. Reprinted by permission of Patti Hare Swensen.

"The Providence of a Tornado," by Harold Funk. Published in a 1934 *Youth's Instructor.* Reprinted by permission of Review and Herald® Publishing Association, Silver Spring, MD 20904. If anyone can provide information about the author or the author's next of kin, please send it to Joe Wheeler (P.O. Box 1246, Conifer, CO 80433).

"Prayer in Extremity," by John Van Ess. Published in W. A. Spicer's book, *The Hand That Intervenes* (Washington, DC: Review and Herald® Publishing Association, 1918). Original text owned by Joe Wheeler.

"Choose Life," by Kathleen Ruckman. Copyright © 2002. Printed by permission of the author.

SECTION FOUR

"Number Two," author unknown. Published in *Review and Herald,* January 12, 1939. Reprinted by permission of Review and Herald® Publishing Association, Silver Spring, MD 20904 If anyone can provide information about the author or the author's next of kin, please send it to Joe Wheeler (P.O. Box 1246, Conifer, CO 80433).

"God, Thank You for Helping Me Hit the Sheriff's Car With a Package of Frozen Meat," by Steve Hamilton. Copyright © 2012. Printed by permission of the author.

"A Father's Prayer," author unknown. Originally published in *Evangelical Christian,* n.d. Republished in *The Review and Herald,* July 14, 1932. Reprinted by permission of Review and Herald® Publishing Association, Silver Spring, MD 20904. If anyone can provide information about the author or the author's next of kin, please send it to Joe Wheeler (P.O. Box 1246, Conifer, CO 80433).

"Sophie and Her God," by Mark O. Prentiss. Originally published in *The Pictorial Review,* n.d. Republished in *The Youth's Instructor,* May 1, 1923. Reprinted by permission of Review and Herald® Publishing Association, Silver Spring, MD 20904. If anyone can provide information about the author or the author's next of kin, please send it to Joe Wheeler (P.O. Box 1246, Conifer, CO 80433).

"The Prayer Quilt," by Velda Anderson. Published in *The Youth's Instructor,* February 11, 1941. Reprinted by permission of Review and Herald® Publishing Association, Silver Spring, MD 20904. If anyone can provide information about the author or the author's next of kin, please send it to Joe Wheeler (P.O. Box 1246, Conifer, CO 80433).

"The Miracle of the Two Blue Coats," by B. Lyn Behrens. Published in *Adventist Review,* September 3, 1998. Reprinted by permission of B. Lyn Behrens.

"The Great Prayer Warrior: George Müller, by A. T. Pierson and Charles Inglis. Published in W. A. Spicer's *The Hand That Intervenes.* Original text owned by Joe Wheeler.

SECTION FIVE
"The Rugged Land," by Juanita Tyson-Flyn. Published in *The Youth's Instructor,* May 20, 1958. Reprinted by permission of Review and Herald® Publishing Association, Silver Spring, MD 20904. If anyone can provide information about the author or the author's next of kin, please send it to Joe Wheeler (P.O. Box 1246, Conifer, CO 80433).

"Ask in Faith, Nothing Wavering," by Adelma Gladys Bates. Published in *The Youth's Instructor,* December 9, 1947. Reprinted by permission of Review and Herald® Publishing Association, Silver Spring, MD 20904. If anyone can provide information about the author or the author's next of kin, please send it to Joe Wheeler (P.O. Box 1246, Conifer, CO 80433).

"One More Prayer for Jennie," by Jewell Johnson. Printed by permission of the author.

"Saved by a Song," as told to Robert Strickland. Published in *The Youth's Instructor,* October 1, 1929. Reprinted by permission of Review and Herald® Publishing Association, Silver Spring, MD 20904. If anyone can provide information about the author or the author's next of kin, please send it to Joe Wheeler (P.O. Box 1246, Conifer, CO 80433).

"Providence on Pitcairn," by Roy P. Clark. Published in *The Youth's Instructor,* September 30, 1947. Reprinted by permission of Review and Herald® Publishing Association, Silver Spring, MD 20904. If anyone can provide information about the author or the author's next of kin, please send it to Joe Wheeler (P.O. Box 1246, Conifer, CO 80433).

"The Little Anchor," author unknown. Published in *The Youth's Instructor,* November 8, 1927. Reprinted by permission of Review and Herald® Publishing Association, Silver Spring, MD 20904. If anyone can provide information about the author or the author's next of kin, please send it to Joe Wheeler (P.O. Box 1246, Conifer, CO 80433).

"A Perfect Mistake," by Cheryl Walterman Stewart. Published in *Live,* July 30, 1989, and in *Christian Reader,* March/April 1998. If anyone can provide information about the author, please send it to Joe Wheeler (P.O. Box 1246, Conifer, CO 80433).